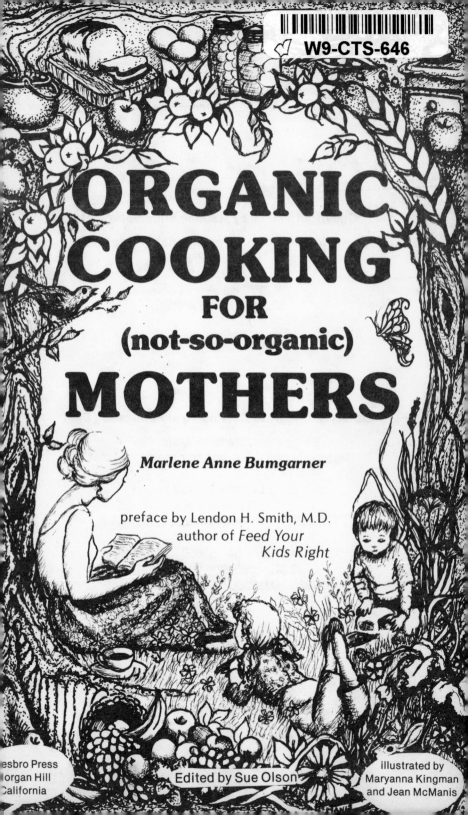

ORGANIC COOKING
FOR
(not-so-organic)
MOTHERS

Marlene Anne Bumgarner

preface by Lendon H. Smith, M.D.
author of *Feed Your
Kids Right*

esbro Press
Morgan Hill
California

Edited by Sue Olson

illustrated by
Maryanna Kingman
and Jean McManis

Special thanks to Sue Olson,
without whom this book would
never have been written.

Library of Congress Cataloging in Publication Data:

Bumgarner, Marlene Anne, 1947—
Organic cooking for (not-so-organic) mothers.

Bibliography: P. 157
Includes index.
1. Cookery (Natural foods)   2. Nutrition.
I. Title
TX741.B85   641.5′637   80-23089
ISBN   0938006-00-2 (spiral)
ISBN   0938006-01-0 (perfectbound)

ISBN 0-938006-00-2 (spiral)
ISBN 0-938006-01-0 (pbk)

Printed in the United States of America.

TABLE OF CONTENTS

PREFACE

Marlene is obviously an expert. She has studied the subject. She has the happy combination of an easy, humorous style and the expertise that comes after study and experience. She has been in the kitchen, and the garden, and the co-op, and the health food store.

She tells us the reasons why her book should be studied and the principles adhered to. She makes sense and she is logical. One finds oneself saying "Ahah, that is why!" She knows not everyone will follow her ideas because many of us are not motivated. Her clear, explicit writing prevents us from saying, "It sounds too difficult." But Marlene has done it and she lets the reader know that it isn't all that tough.

Thank you, Marlene, for making health easier.

Lendon H. Smith, M.D.

INTRODUCTION

IT'S NOT ALL WHEAT GERM AND BREWER'S YEAST

Recently I overheard my daughter talking with a school friend. Doña Ana said, smugly I thought, "My mommy only cooks natural foods." Her friend wanted to know what that meant. "Oh, they're things you buy in a health food store," was the answer.

I cringed a little when I heard that. The more I thought about it, however, the more I realized that to people who are unfamiliar with natural foods, it probably does seem as if we eat a limited fare, consisting entirely of health food items like wheat germ, brewer's yeast, and blackstrap molasses. Not true.

First of all, let it go on record that I like to eat. It is also a fact that I like to cook. However, I have to include in my cooking considerations two somewhat picky children, a man who works an hour's commute from our home, and my own full time job.

As if that were not enough, we are far from rich, and could not afford to buy all of our food in specialty shops even if we wanted to. We buy most of our staples from food co-operatives and natural food stores, but fruits, vegetables and meat usually come from supermarkets. We use our slow cooker, a blender, a refrigerator, and a freezer to process and store our foods, just like most of today's suburban families.

Yet we eat almost entirely natural foods. What do I mean by that? Most of all I mean that I read every label before buying food, and veto almost everything that contains BHA, BHT, sodium nitrate, sodium nitrite, artificial coloring, artificial flavoring, monosodium glutamate, or words that read like a prescription (sure, some of those additives have been "shown to be safe", but I don't know what most of them are, and anyway, who needs them?) I also veto foods which have refined sugar (dextrose, sucrose, glucose, fructose, corn syrup) in the first three ingredients, indicating that they are major components of the food.

Yet we eat good food, tasty food. And we are far from going hungry for lack of packaged cake mixes, puddings, top-of-the-stove hamburger flavorings or prepared soup. Instead of artificially colored, artificially flavored, sugar-heavy drink mixes that turn their lips red, our children enjoy lemonade made with real lemons and honey. Or grape juice made from real grapes. Instead of eating packaged casserole flavorings my children help me smash sage and dill and chop vegetables

2

to put in our dinner. And instead of colored, sugared, and flavored nutritional nothings for breakfast, accompanied by artifical orange juice, they choose from fresh fruit, whole grain cereal or eggs most mornings, and whole grain pancakes or waffles on weekends, washed down with pure fruit juice, sometimes even squozen fresh.

So *now* who's being smug? I'm not, really, because here and there is a stick of gum, a cookie eaten just an hour before dinner, or a fruit punch slipped in right under my nose because I'm too tired to say no. But then eating natural foods isn't a religion with us, either, but rather a style; a pattern; a habit. If most of the time, most of the food we eat is free from artificial things, then that leaves our bodies freer to deal with the toxins we do throw into them occasionally. Even I now and then snack on a candy bar, eat at a hamburger parlor, or enjoy a soft drink.

But most of the time, most of the food we eat is real food, whole food, without any of its parts taken away, and without anything artificial added. And most of the time, it tastes pretty good.

THAT'S REALLY ORGANIC!

The expressions "natural foods" and "organic foods" get tossed around a lot, and those people who try to eat naturally often use the words interchangeably, along with "health foods", "whole foods", and "real food", to the thorough confusion of everyone concerned. What ARE these things? Does it really make any difference whether your vegetables were fertilized, sprayed, milled, or flavored before you ate them? The entire subject of food growing, processing, and selling is fraught with confusion, the result of a trend toward eating unadulterated foods in a society where until recently almost all food products were chemically colored, flavored, scented, coated, or packaged.

More people are reading labels, asking questions, writing letters, and putting pressure on the food industry to provide them with food that is unprocessed, in its natural "from the farm" form, and free from pesticide residue. While traditional dieticians, food chemists, and even medical doctors protest that you can't alter the vitamin content of an apple by growing it organically, still thousands of people have altered their buying patterns to purchase their food from co-operatives, organic groceries, and stores specializing in locally grown, unsprayed, and unprocessed produce and grains.

Why? Syndicated columnists write, chiding the so-called health food faddists, that there has never been an authenticated case of illness resulting directly from pesticide residues, and that such "natural" foods as mushrooms, potatoes, and lima beans often contain poisonous substances (microscopic amounts of arsenic, hydrogen cyanide). Yet research findings from numerous experiments have shown the toxicity of pesticide residue over a long period of time on animals, and Michael F. Jacobson, the author of *Eater's Digest, The Consumer's Factbook of Food Additives*, cites many cases of accidental poisoning or illness caused by such additives as monosodium glutamate (msg) and sodium nitrate.

Mothers of hyperactive children all over the country have attested to the negative effects of artificial coloring, flavoring, and preservatives on their children's behavior. Cancer is becoming an issue of major proportions; several studies link it to additives. My reply is, why *not*? Why *not* try to eat food which is unprocessed, providing us with higher amounts of the vitamins, minerals, and fibers which are present in nature? Why *not* avoid additives and processed foods? Why *not* try, whenever possible, to eat fruits and vegetables which we have grown ourselves on pesticide-free soil, or which was at least grown without chemical treatment? Why *not*? But that still leaves us in this morass of confusing terms. Organic, natural, unprocessed — what does it all mean?

In search of clarity, then, let us do a little defining. The word ORGANIC is short for organically grown, which generally refers to food grown on or in soil which has not been chemically fertilized and which has not been sprayed or treated with pesticides, fungicides, or hormones. Some crops are commercially fertilized but not sprayed, and are therefore not strictly organic, but I prefer them to regular commercial crops. Obviously, the number of food crops which are completely organically grown in this country is very small. They tend to be the products of home gardens and small truck farms, and can be found in only a limited number of fruit and vegetable stands and natural food stores with produce sections.

NATURAL FOODS include organically grown foods, but also include many others — fruits, vegetables, grains, flours, nuts, seeds, dairy products, juices, herbs, spices — which do not contain artificial flavorings, chemically derived artificial colorings, or preservatives. They may be the result of crops which were chemically fertilized, and sometimes even of crops which were sprayed with pesticides, but wherever possible natural foods processors purchase organically grown food. Natural foods also include prepared food items, such as soups, baked goods, condiments, fruit butters, beverages and desserts, made without artificial additives. As often as possible natural foods are made with whole grain flours rather than refined, with honey instead of sugar, and with vegetable coloring rather than chemical.

The term HEALTH FOOD has been around for a long time. The traditional emphasis in health food stores has been on supernutrition, and the proportion of vitamin supplements to food is usually much higher than will be found in natural food stores. Another distinction is that specialized food needed by people with dietary limitations, such as diabetics, post-cardiac surgery patients, and hypoglycemics, is classified as health food. According to the code of ethics of a regional group of the National Nutritional Foods Association, no member will "knowingly sell or supply those foods that contain harmful chemical food additives or artificial ingredients that are alien to the recognized concept of natural foods, nor . . . knowingly deal in products that are untruthfully labeled." Most owners of health food stores are members of the NNFA or a similar organization, and so try to meet these standards. By this description, then, there is little difference between nutritional (health) foods and natural foods.

Stores which try to avoid the almost religious fervor which often accompanies the "health food" label and the hippie appearance of many "natural foods" establishments, have occasionally coined their

6

own expressions to explain what sort of foods lie inside their doors. Such creations are "Good Earth Products", "Whole Foods", and "Real Food", all alluding to the fact that the food sold there is complete, unrefined, and has little or nothing added to change its color, flavor, or texture.

Armed with these definitions, then, how does one go about redirecting eating patterns to incorporate these "new" kinds of foods? I recently read an amusing book by Jane Kinderlehrer, former Senior Editor of *Prevention* Magazine. In her book, *Confessions of a Sneaky Organic Cook*, she presents a case for being something less than honest in preparing natural foods for her family.

"Why be sneaky? ... Because, at certain stages of their growth and development (like from toddlers through teens and right up to the coronary stage) anything that smacks of 'health' is considered square, for the birds, when they get sophisticated, 'faddist'."

Surely you have experienced the same kind of trouble with some of the people you cook for. The surest way to turn off a small child is to tell her to eat her vegetables because they're good for her. In the same manner, a slice of whole wheat bread becomes less palatable the moment it is described as "healthy".

So go easy on your family. Especially if natural foods are new to you, don't, please, go home from your first night in a natural foods cooking class, or from a lecture, or after reading this book, and prepare an entire meal of unfamiliar health food dishes. They won't get eaten, and your family just might respond by going out for hamburgers.

Change your eating patterns gradually. Instead of making a batch of whole wheat muffins or pancakes for a family which has been used to Aunt Jemima, try using your usual mix and adding just a tablespoon or so of wheat germ or whole wheat pastry flour, increasing the liquid a little to make up for it. Or make some from scratch, substituting whole wheat flour for only a quarter of the flour in the recipe, then working up to more.

You can increase the nutritional content of your puddings, baked goods, beverages, and lots of other foods by adding extra powdered milk to the recipe. Don't use the puffed-up heat processed variety, though. Buy spray processed milk powder and you will get far more vitamins and minerals. When mixed in a blender, noninstant powdered milk is no more lumpy than the instant type, and the low temperature method of processing leaves in more natural nutrition. Spray processed powdered milk can now be purchased in both instant and noninstant forms. (See the section on Milk for more details.)

I stir a few tablespoons of powdered milk into each half-gallon of raw milk I buy; a teaspoon or two into each cup of yoghurt; a quarter cup extra into each quart of "milkshake". (The milkshakes at our house, by the way, are just as much in demand as those from the hamburger stands, yet they are entirely different. With practice, you can make milkshakes just as thick and creamy as the commercial kind without the use of chemical emulsifiers or stabilizers, and if you use fresh sweet fruit you can make them entirely without sugar. We combine fresh fruit and milk with lecithin, whey, and protein powder.)

Wheat germ can also be sneaked into many of your meals without setting off a revolution. Although not quite so nutritious as whole wheat flour, its vitamin content adds a lot to baked goods, hot or cold cereal or other dishes. Grind some in your blender, a cup at a time, until the texture is like flour, and you can add as much as a quarter cup to a packaged cake mix (until you stop using such things entirely). Use wheat germ instead of flour to thicken gravies or casseroles, or soups. Slip it into pancake recipes, or bread, or sprinkle it on French toast or even cinnamon toast (try making cinnamon toast with whole wheat bread instead of white, and with honey instead of sugar — it's great).

There are lots of ways to sneak nutrition into the food of an unsuspecting family. For the smaller children you can freeze yoghurt in paper cups (the commercial frozen yoghurt, alas, usually has artificial coloring and lots of sugar). Flavor the yoghurt yourself with fresh fruit puree and sweeten it with a touch of honey. Or you can freeze unsweetened fruit juices in plastic molds or ice cube trays for popsicles. Yoghurt popsicles can be made by stirring a little milk into the yoghurt before freezing, and they will freeze harder.

Try some of these nutritious tricks and others to follow on your family, and enjoy feeling good about the improvement in their diet while feeling a little bit sneaky, too.

STAPLES FOR AN ORGANIC KITCHEN

Don't run out and buy all these at once, but try as much as possible to stock up on small quantities of each of the following things: (Items marked with a star should be refrigerated in airtight containers.)

Whole wheat flour*
Cracked wheat*
Brown rice
Undegerminated cornmeal*
Wheat germ*
Miller's bran (wheat bran)
Carob powder
Raw honey
Raw sunflower seeds*
Unhulled sesame seeds
Unrefined vegetable oils*
Raw nuts*
Seeds for sprouting
Molasses
Pure maple syrup
Soybeans, soy grits* and soy flour*

Try to stop buying the things on this list. Times being what they are, I certainly don't recommend you throw out all that you have, but gradually eliminate them from your meals.

All purpose white flour
White sugar
White rice
Packaged mixes (cake, sauce, salad dressing) which contain BHA, BHT
Anything containing artificial coloring or flavoring
Anything with sugar (or one of its forms) in the first three ingredients
Synthetic sweeteners or products sweetened with them

WHAT'S THIS IN MY POTATO CHIPS?

READING LABELS — CHEMICAL AND NATURAL INGREDIENTS TO KNOW

What goes into our food? A few generations ago, that question could be answered quite simply. Salt, pepper, some herbs, perhaps, but few people ate food that they didn't grow, or at least that wasn't grown nearby, and no one struggled with labels containing multisyllabic words that would baffle college graduates.

Now that our food is grown in agricultural areas, picked and shipped to specialized plants for washing and packing, then sent to distant places for distribution, we have many more ingredients to consider. At the very least we have the possibilities of chemical residues from sprays used on the crops to reduce damage from bugs and diseases. At the worst we have a combination of chemical residues and chemicals which have been added to preserve color, add color, enhance flavor, change flavor, keep food soft and fresh looking, prevent separation, delay rancidity.

So we make the decision to use no more packaged food, to grow as many of our vegetables and fruits as we can, and to obtain the rest from farmers who do not use sprays. We enter the doors of a natural food store, looking for some products to fill out our now barren cupboards. What do we see on the shelves? Wheat germ. Brewer's yeast. Blackstrap molasses. Tofu. Bran. What ARE these things?

Leaving packaged food behind can be frightening, especially when the alternatives are so unfamiliar. So in this section we have collected some of the major items you will want to learn about — some to avoid, some to use. References to a variety of ingredients are scattered throughout the book, and a list of staples and sources is in the Appendix. But this section is a good place to start.

PRESERVATIVES

In a recent conversation with a friend I mentioned our family's ban on food containing BHA and BHT, two overused chemical preservatives. Her reply astounded me. "What's the point," she said, "of reading hundreds of package labels in order to avoid the two or three that contain tiny amounts of a preservative?

I have, as I write this, seven items on my desk: a box of popular cold cereal, an envelope of fortified milk flavoring, one strip of active dry yeast packets, flavored instant gelatin mix, some fudge brownie mix, a tin of ready-to-spread chocolate frosting, and a can of orange-flavored instant coffee. All contain butylated hydroxyanisole (BHA). All were located in my friend's kitchen.

According to Michael Jacobson (*Eater's Digest: The Consumer's Factbook of Food Additives*), "Butylated hydroxyanisole and butylated hydroxytoluene (BHA and BHT) have not been adequately tested, accumulate in body fat, and are actually superfluous in many of the foods in which they are used. They certainly cannot be 'generally recognized as safe' . . . Until their safety is established, they should be barred from food."

BHA and BHT are only two of the additives which are consistently put into our food, but they are easily avoidable. The reason this is true, ironically, is that in most cases these additives are not necessary for the function they are supposed to be serving. BHA and BHT are antioxidants; they may prevent polyunsaturated oils from becoming rancid; they may also protect the fat-soluble vitamins (A, D, E). Yet numerous manufacturers produce food items such as those mentioned above without feeling the necessity of these antioxidants in their formulas.

Why, then, do manufacturers put these ingredients into our food? The original justification for introducing food additives was that they would benefit us — the consumers — by improving the nutritional quality, the aesthetic appearance, the keepability, or the convenience of the foods in question. Yet some manufacturers of vegetable oil, of potato chips, and of baking yeast use BHA in their products; others do not. The ones who do may be doing so, according to Jacobson, simply out of habit, or due to outmoded manufacturing techniques, or to slightly extend the shelf life of their products (do you have any idea how old those crackers were that you bought last week?), but the indications are strong that they have no really good reason for their practice.

What are the dangers from ingesting BHA and BHT? Beatrice Trum Hunter, in her *Fact Book on Food Additives and Your Health*, reports that various experiments with animals have demonstrated such effects as metabolic stress, depression of growth rate, loss of weight, increase of liver weight, damage to the liver and kidneys, increase of serum cholesterol and phospholid levels, baldness, and fetal abnormalities in offspring such as failure to develop normal eyes, from the storage of BHT in animal tissues, fats, and organs. Jacobson reviews the research history of BHA and BHT in his book and concludes that scientists have spent lots of energy on studies to determine whether these antioxidants interfere with animal reproduction, but little or no effort to determine whether they cause cancer.

Whether or not BHA and BHT have been proven dangerous, the fact remains that they have not been proven safe, and that they probably are not as necessary as food manufacturers would like us to believe for their product integrity. These additives are now found in breakfast cereals, chewing gum, packaged convenience dinners, vegetable oils, shortening, potato flakes, potato chips, enriched rice, cake and frosting mixes, candy, and countless other oil-containing products.

So what do we do? Do we stop eating butter because we read somewhere that they are putting BHA in the natural food coloring, carotene? Do we stop eating gelatine desserts? Instant coffee? Cakes made from mixes?

I tend to hover between yes and no. We should all start reading labels more carefully, and comparing different brands of similar products. Look at your own eating patterns, and see how far you are willing to go. In our house it was easy to give up cake mixes and ready-to-spread frosting because I always made those things from scratch anyway. I was stumped when I first discovered BHA in my baking yeast, but sought (and found) two brands which didn't.

Salad oils should say "no preservatives" right on the labels, otherwise they are suspect. I prefer cold-pressed or unrefined vegetable oils anyway, and they rarely contain extra ingredients.

Flavored gelatin? It isn't difficult to make your own. My feelings about the entire range of boxed breakfast cereals is negative. How about making your own granola, or muesli, or cooking cracked grains on cold mornings? In addition to avoiding preservatives, you'll save money.

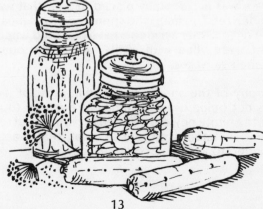

Potato chips, stove-top convenience dinners, pancake mixes, and packaged soups? All of these are available without preservatives. Of course we should strive to cook as many of our meals as possible from fresh raw ingredients so that we know exactly what we are getting, but when the time comes for assistance from the packaging industry, the products are there — you have only to seek them out and insist on them. Our grocers will respond to our buying practices. An example is the effect of the nitrate boycott.

Many children are growing up without taking bologna sandwiches in their lunchboxes, without linking the taste of hot dogs and mustard to baseball season. A growing number of mothers refuse to buy ham or bacon, and not for religious reasons.

What is happening? I know many families who eat no lunchmeat, no hot dogs, no ham, no bacon. My own children don't ask for salami sandwiches or hot dogs — we've never eaten them at home. I, too, have avoided supermarket lunchmeat, ham, bacon, frankfurters.

The reason is potassium nitrate — saltpeter. Those of you who know American history are aware that saltpeter was an essential ingredient in Revolutionary War gunpowder. You may not be aware that it is now an overwhelmingly common ingredient in cold cuts and cured meat. Other forms of the same ingredient are sodium nitrite, sodium nitrate, and potassium nitrite. These food additives are alternately known as "preservatives" and "color preservers", depending unto whom you are speaking. According to Michael Jacobson, nitrite is one of the most toxic chemicals in our food supply.

Our bodies convert nitrates to nitrites, and nitrite combines with the red blood cells, potentially in sufficient quantity to limit the oxygen-carrying power of the hemoglobin. Not only are nitrates dangerous when included in our food intentionally, however, nitrates are so poisonous that their very presence in food-preparation areas leads to the potential for fatal accidents. Jacobson cites one occasion where nitrate was accidentally placed in a jar that was supposed to contain tenderizer. The man who sprinkled on his meat did not live to find out the error. Other accidents have occurred when salt shakers in a restaurant were filled with nitrite, and when homemakers have overcured their sausages.

The irony of the situation is that in most of its present uses, saltpeter is not being used in sufficient quantity to preserve meat. Ostensibly, the nitrite powder is added to curing meat to kill botulinum, a toxic agent sometimes present in meat, but in actual usage, it is primarily added to keep the color attractive.

In *Housekeeping in Old Virginia*, a delightful compendium of household lore, it says quite clearly, "In order to impart redness to the hams, rub on each a teaspoon of pulverized saltpetre before salting." Salt was the primary preserving agent, and the nitrate was simply a cosmetic ingredient.

What to do? Some manufacturers are now producing salami, bologna, hot dogs, bacon, and sausages without nitrites or nitrates. These meats are darker in color (more natural, remember), and are found in the freezer compartment of your supermarket or health food store. If your grocer doesn't have them, educate him about the difference, and ask him to order some. Health Valley, Jones, Tobin's, and Taste Wright make these products.

Frozen lunch meats should remain frozen until you intend to use them, but then can be kept for two or three days open (reseal in a plastic bag) in your refrigerator. I separate frankfurters into two or three separate bunches when I get home (by which time they are usually loose in the package, but still frozen), and freeze them until needed. Cook a whole pound of bacon at a time, removing the package from the freezer just before cooking, and return cooked bacon to the freezer in plastic bags. It is possible to make your own sausages and beef jerky.

The good news is that enough people have refused to buy lunchmeat with preservatives that now the FDA has reopened research on nitrates.

There are other preservatives that should be watched for, and avoided whenever possible. Unknown quantities of additives are consumed every time we eat a bag of french fries or drink a commercial milk shake, so it is especially important that the food we eat AT HOME be chemical-free.

My recommendation is that you buy a copy of *Eater's Digest* and use it often to check the safety of additives whose names you do not recognize. Another guide to grocery store safety is *The Supermarket Handbook* by Nikki and David Goldbeck. The Goldbeck's have done an excellent job of cataloguing things to look for when buying food, and provide a good reference for the novice natural foods cook.

A GERM OF WHEAT

When a grain of wheat is milled into flour, into the white flour which is used in practically every commercially-produced baked good and almost every kitchen in the country, the embryo, or germ, of the grain is removed along with the hull and the bran. For many years this residue was sold for nearly nothing to animal feed producers. Now, however, we pay up to a dollar a pound for fresh wheat germ at health food stores.

Why the switch? The earliest flour mills pulverized the germ right along with the starchy part, releasing the vitamin-rich wheat germ oil into the flour, coloring and flavoring it slightly. Although this seems desirable to those of us seeking to improve the vitamin and mineral content of our foods, it was not convenient to the grocer or baker, since wheat germ oil soon becomes rancid, and bags of flour left on the shelf for long will spoil. The invention in the mid-nineteenth century of high speed roller mills which separated the germ from the wheat kernel and allowed the germ to be sifted out was considered a great technological advance.

What do we lose by using white flour? After all, it is "all-purpose" and "enriched".

All-purpose means it can be used for breads as well as cakes and pastries. Since the bran and germ have been removed, the differences between hard wheat and softer pastry wheat become academic — everything comes out fluffy and spongy.

Enriched? Well, that means that a few vitamins and minerals (less than a quarter of what were removed) have been added back into the depleted substance. But by eliminating the bran from the flour, we are missing important fibers, and by removing the wheat germ, we are deprived of Vitamin E, vital to the health of our hearts, our endurance, and our tolerance of environmental toxins. Wheat germ also contains protein (24 grams in half a cup), B-complex vitamins, iron, copper, magnesium, manganese, calcium, and phosphorus.

One popular nutrition writer, Paavo Airola, author of *How To Get Well*, feels very strongly that wheat germ is best avoided entirely if the alternative is to eat it when it is over a week old. He contends that rancid wheat germ is a potential carcinogen.

UNREFINED OIL has been cold-pressed, and has also been extracted without the use of solvents. Its flavor is reminiscent of the vegetable from which it was squeezed. The best way to learn which oil tastes best with what is to buy several types — safflower, soybean, olive, corn, for example — and try them. Generally, the same rule works which we use for honey — the lighter the color, the lighter the taste. Use light tasting oils for baking; stronger flavored oils for salads and hot dishes.

There are some places where vegetable oil simply does not work, such as for spreading bread or toast or a fresh, hot, bran muffin. When it comes to making Scottish shortbread, liquid vegetable oil just doesn't provide the same tender texture, and for the flaky pie crust necessary to hold a delicate quiche, I return to butter.

Why butter, instead of margarine? First of all, they are both saturated fats (you can tell because at room temperature they hold their shape), so one doesn't have an advantage there. And both contain incredible numbers of calories. I don't believe in nitpicking ten calories when I'm already sinning.

But most of all, it comes to a basic decision about natural foods. Butter is a natural product; margarine usually a synthetic one. Butter is 100% whole sweet cream; margarine is a collection of saturated and unsaturated vegetable oils, some of which are highly subject to pesticide residues, blended together with chemicals, coloring and flavoring agents, and salt. Butter is just butter.

Be aware of the fact that commercially marketed butter may contain some coloring agents (especially in the winter, when the grain diet of the cows restricts the vitamin A content and the yellow color which goes with it), and usually contains salt. Except for that, most butter is fairly natural.

There are now some brands of margarine available which contain no artificial ingredients. They have some more work to do before they will pass muster at our house as bread spreads, but they do serve well in some uses.

19

An alternative to butter which is a little cheaper, and considerably lower in saturated fat, is to make "Better Butter",* described in *Laurel's Kitchen*, a wonderful book by Laurel Robertson, Bronwen Godfrey, and Carol Flinders. Better Butter is made by softening butter, blending it with an equal quantity of safflower, soy or corn oil, and adding water, powdered milk solids, lecithin and salt. For two cups of Better Butter add 2 tablespoons water, 2 tablespoons powdered milk, ¼ teaspoon lecithin, and ½ teaspoon salt.

Better Butter should be refrigerated between uses, but it does keep well at room temperatures, and can be used in place of margarine in recipes or on bread.

ARTIFICIAL COLORINGS AND FLAVORINGS

When I was in teacher training, we were taught that there was a certain kind of "problem child" known as a hyperkinetic, or hyperactive, individual. When I began teaching, I worked for a semester with an eight year old boy who was so described, and discovered the disability that a nearly nonexistant attention span, low frustration tolerance, and inability to screen out distraction, can be.

Parents of these so-called hyperactive children waver between exhaustion and depression — exhaustion because their children may have low sleep requirements, and leave materials strewn in the wake of their constant search for new activities, and depression because they fear that this will go on forever, that their child will not learn to read, will be kicked out of school for refusing to settle down, will wander off into trouble from boredom.

It is no wonder, then, that a doctor who professes to have a solution to the problem would be hailed as a messiah. Dr. Ben Feingold, a San Francisco allergist, published a book, *Why Your Child is Hyperactive*, in 1974 to spread his findings that diet can influence activity levels in some children. Many parents after reading his book have tried his recommended food program, and enough are seeing satisfactory results that support groups are appearing all over the country. Feingold Association meetings are places for mothers of hyperactive children to go to learn about their children's problem, the Feingold K-P Diet, and to get specific suggestions to help them put it in practice.

---

*Used with permission.

Feingold's belief is that artificial colorings, artificial flavorings, preservatives, and some naturally occurring salicylates contribute to the symptoms of hyperkinesis as well as to some learning disabilities, allergies, asthma, rashes, hives, and nasal congestions. By removing these items from the diets of children struggling with these problems, Dr. Feingold reports, significant improvements can often be seen.

My son John, while an amazingly active child, has never been classified hyperactive. He had sufficient attention span at the age of two to take all the tissues out of a kleenex box, one at a time, and stuff them into the toilet. Even he, however, suffers from the effects of some colorings and flavorings. Decongestants in sugar syrup give him a rash; the same chemical in pure form causes no reaction. I can tell within minutes of his return from a walk with his grandmother if she has succumbed to his pleas for a raspberry popsicle or a cherry slush cone — he will alternate between yawns and temper tantrums for the next two hours.

So far no one has duplicated Feingold's results in scientific studies, primarily because it is very difficult to control the eating habits of school-aged hyperactive children if they are not already on a structured eating plan. Yet this lack of scientific support for his diet doesn't stop the hundreds of parents who are forming Feingold Associations all over the country, who are lobbying for less junk food in school lunch areas, and who are willing to talk at length to anyone who asks about the changes in their lives which have come about since they altered their children's diets.

I think Dr. Feingold's research has a day-to-day meaning for all of us who deal with children, whether we be parents, teachers, or camp counselors. If there really are results to be seen when additives are removed from a hyperactive child's diet, it seems reasonable that there is some benefit to removing them from everyone's diet. Perhaps the threshold has not been reached by all of us, but it is most certainly there.

According to Michael Jacobson (*Eater's Digest*), the average American consumes about five pounds of chemical food additives each year. Many of these additives are safe, and some are probably necessary for the production and packaging of our food, but many others are unnecessary. Some are certainly harmful.

Using the result of Ben Feingold's diet as a clue, I think it may be valuable for our health and longevity to return to a diet which is free from as many additives as possible. This can be done fairly simply by avoiding prepared, so-called "convenience foods", and by reading labels and rejecting products with artificial colors, artificial flavors, preservatives or other chemicals. Good references for the safety of individual additives are *Eater's Digest: The Consumer's Factbook of Food Additives* by Michael Jacobson, and *Supermarket Handbook,* by Nikki and David Goldbeck.

Avoiding artificial colorings will require a real effort at first. Read the label on anything you buy. Soft drinks, powdered drink mixes, gelatin desserts — popular summer thirst quenchers — are loaded with sugar, with colorings, with flavorings, with preservatives.

Soup mixes, cake mixes, canned fruit cocktail — for a while it will seem that everything has been colored or flavored, preserved or stabilized. But colored sodas can be replaced with fruit juice and sparkling mineral water; soups can be made ahead and frozen. Fresh fruit, fresh juice and homemade baked goods taste far better than canned goods, and cost less too. But even if some of the alternatives you find are more expensive, I think you will agree that the peace of mind is worth the extra money.

22

CAROB — ST. JOHN'S BREAD

Carob is one of those mysterious foods which has been given the golden seal of virtue by the health food industry, and thus encouraged thousands of people to partake of its flavor and healthgiving properties without really knowing why.

Unfortunately, that is often the case with natural foods. They live or die in our mass buying economy for reasons usually more related to their packaging or sales image than to their food value.

Carob powder is ground from the dried pods of the carob tree. The powder is sometimes called carob flour, and sometimes called St. John's Bread. To further the confusion, the seeds inside the pod are known as locust beans. The outside layer of the seeds is made into a gummy substance which was once used to glue mummy bindings together, and is now used as a stabilizer in ice cream, salad dressing, pie filling, and various sauces (it's usually listed on the label as locust bean gum).

To make carob powder, the pods are roasted and dried, then broken into several pieces. The bitter seeds are discarded, and the pieces then ground in a flour mill. The resulting powder can be used to flavor your baked goods with a subtle, cinnamon/chocolate-like taste, and to add color as well as flavor to some breads. In significant quantities, carob has a gentle laxative effect, but in the amounts used in baking, that is usually not noticeable.

Carob powder is generally presented in health food stores as an alternative to chocolate, although the flavors are far from identical. Still, they are somewhat similar, and most children enjoy milk flavored with honey and carob powder just as much as they ever liked hot chocolate. Chocolate has several bad marks against it — it contains caffeine, it is a common allergen, it inhibits calcium absorption, and it has an extremely high fat content.

Carob powder is a fairly nutritious and tasty food. It contains a little bit of protein, not too much fat, and a fair number of minerals (primarily calcium).

However, in all fairness, I must point out that the least healthy thing about chcolate is the way it is used — in sweetened milk drinks and candy bars, thick desserts and oversweet baked goods — and carob can be used in exactly the same ways. When it is, it loses some of its advantages over chocolate.

Fortunately, since carob contains a lot of natural sugar, it doesn't require much additional sweetening to taste good. Also fortunately, since carob is promoted by the health food industry, even the candy bars made with it usually contain very little in the way of additives or harmful ingredients. But it is STILL candy. The flavored milk powder contains sugar, even if it is brown sugar, and the carob chips contain sugar, and the carob malt balls contain sugar, and the carob covered peanuts contain sugar. . . .

Our families' approach to carob has been to use it in moderation where we might have used chocolate before — on cold nights, stirred into hot milk, for example, or blended with cream cheese and honey for a cake icing. Since we do have a chocolate allergy among us, we don't buy chocolate at all, but leave the satisfaction of secret binges to those who can obtain it outside of the house!

BRAN, FIBER, AND HOW TO GET IT

A few years ago, dietary fiber was one of the most popular subjects around. Books appeared on the subject weekly, doctors prescribed visits to health food stores, and the market on unprocessed miller's bran boomed. Then, like so many food fads, bran lost its place in the media and most people forgot about it.

Just what IS dietary fiber? And what is bran? Dietary fiber is not a new subject. Remember when your grandmother used to urge everyone to finish their vegetables, saying "You need your roughage!"? Fiber, roughage, bulk — it's the cellulose, the extra skins and strings and hulls of foods that we don't digest and convert into useful proteins or carbohydrates, but which serve the extremely important function of pushing waste materials through the intestinal tract, thereby shortening the amount of time that wastes are stored in the body.

So what? Who cares how long it takes to eliminate leftover dinner? Apparently, we all do, or at least we all should. Observation of other cultures, their eating habits and their states of health, and research among Europeans and Americans has caused numerous doctors to state that the reduction of fiber from the diet increases the incidence of several diseases and conditions, among which are cancer of the colon, cancer of the rectum, appendicitis, diverticulitis, phlebitis, ischemic heart disease, and obesity.

The relationship of dietary fiber to each of these problems is slightly different, but basically the idea is that if food wastes lie too long in the intestinal tract, numerous difficulties can result. Fecal material loses moisture and becomes more difficult to pass, injuring the colon and the rectum and setting the stage for later infections. Cholesterol elimination is reduced by the amount of cholesterol which is broken down and reabsorbed into the bloodstream from the intestines. And the size of the colon is gradually decreased, leading to difficulties in later life.

The complex relationships between fiber and disease are thoroughly discussed in *The Save Your Life Diet*, by David Reuben, M.D. He discusses specifics, gives references, and suggests ways each of us can increase our intake of dietary fiber.

One of the simplest ways is to add bran to your diet. Whole grains are one of the richest sources of fiber, but by the time they have been milled into the all-purpose flour, polished rice, pearled barley, and degerminated cornmeal which appear in grocery stores, most of their fiber has been removed.

It is possible to purchase grains such as rice, barley, rye, millet and wheat in their whole form in the health food section of large supermarkets or in natural food stores, and whole grain flours should be substituted for white whenever possible.

It is also possible to buy the bran which has been removed from grains of wheat and rice from the same sources. Bran is cheap, usually less than 50 cents a pound, and can be sprinkled on cereal, stirred into sauces and gravies, and added to meat loaf, hamburger, and casseroles.

The author of *The Book of Bran*, Carlson Wade, emphasizes that a few tablespoons of bran a day will not alone solve the fiber deficiency in the Western diet, although it will certainly improve the situation. He quotes Dr. Benjamin H. Ershoff of the Loma Linda University School of Medicine as saying "Dietary fiber is not an inert substance which passes unchanged through the gastro-intestinal tract, but a group of compounds that play an important role in the maintenance of health. Different fibers have different activities and different effects."

Other foods which need to be included in our diet to balance the fiber intake include nuts, seeds, beans, fruits and vegetables (the last two with skins included whenever possible, such as when they are from known organic sources). These fiber-rich foods fit well into an eating pattern of snacking, buffet, or catch-as-catch-can. Snack mixes containing raw nuts, flake coconut, raisins and chopped dates can be refrigerated in large containers, and scooped into a serving bowl on a moment's notice; apple wedges, orange segments and strips of banana make an attractive edible centerpiece; stir-fried vegetables served over a bed of brown rice can stand alone or accompany a meat entree.

Our traditional eating patterns, leaning heavily on meat, refined starches (white rice, white flour, degerminated corn), and overcooked vegetables, will have to change before we can consider ourselves a really healthy nation. Why not start by adding more fiber to each meal you eat?

One of our favorite ways to add fiber to our breakfasts is with bran muffins:

HONEY-BRAN MUFFINS

2 cups whole wheat pastry flour
1½ cup miller's bran
¼ cup wheat germ
½ teaspoon salt
1½ teaspoon baking soda
½ teaspoon grated nutmeg
¼ cup brown sesame seeds
½ cup orange or apple juice
2 cups buttermilk or kefir
1 beaten egg
½ cup honey or molasses
2 tablespoons light vegetable oil

Stir together dry ingredients; blend liquid ingredients in a bowl or a blender and stir gently into dry. Pour into greased muffin tins — about eighteen — and bake for 25 minutes at 350 F.

Let cool slightly, twist to remove from muffin tins, and serve hot, split, with butter.

Variation:

Add one cup of variously chopped fruit and nuts, such as chopped apples, raisins, dates, blueberries, almonds, sunflower seeds, or pecans. You'll get 22 to 24 muffins that way.

BAKING POWDER DOESN'T ALWAYS COME IN A CAN

I am often asked how to make baking powder. Since many of us grew up without knowing we *could* even make our own, and have done all of our baking with commercial products, let me begin by describing how leavening agents work, and then get into the different kinds that are available.

Baking soda, one of the earliest leavening agents to be commercially produced, works by simply releasing carbon dioxide into your batter when the soda is mixed with an acid (buttermilk, vinegar, molasses or fruit juice for example). Although long used and well accepted, baking soda (bicarbonate of soda) is now thought by some people to be hard on the digestive system as well as destructive of B vitamins, and is being used less than it used to be.

Baking powder also works on the carbon dioxide principle, which is not too surprising, since one of its ingredients is baking soda. However, in order to give us some control over the amount of leavening, the acid is provided right in the mixture, along with a starch to keep the powder from absorbing moisture. Since the baking powder requires liquid to work, absorbing moisture does more than just cause the stuff to cake up; it also sets up a premature activity in the can, weakening the results later in your baked goods.

There are basically three types of baking powder. The one most of us are familiar with us is double-acting, or sodium aluminum sulfate (SAS)-Phosphate. This one only releases a small amount of the carbon dioxide at room temperature — the baked goods need to be put into the oven for the remainder to be freed.

Double-acting baking powder has been very popular since it was formulated, partly at least because you may make up a batter of biscuits, pancakes, or whatever, and refrigerate it until needed. However, residues of sodium aluminum sulfate are now thought to be unhealthy for us. I don't know any scientist who has come right out and said that aluminum is bad for us, but test animals have shown some severe damage when aluminum salts were included in their diets, and enough nutritional writers have shown uncertainty about the subject to convince me to change from double-acting baking powder to one of the others, the so-called "fast acting" varieties.

Phosphate baking powder uses calcium acid phosphate to combine with baking soda to form its carbon dioxide. Common brands of phosphate powders are Rumford, Jewel, and Dr. Price (Magic baking powder in Canada). About half or a little more of the gas is released at room temperature when combined with liquids, and the rest releases in the oven. This is a good substitute for the double-acting kind, because it is the slower of the fast-acting types.

Tartrate baking powder, however, is coming back into vogue because of its more "natural" acid, tartaric acid, which is a byproduct of wine making. (I hear chemists berating me that chemicals are "natural", but I'm merely quoting my friends.) When you buy natural grape juice at a health food store you may notice crystals at the bottom of the bottle; those are tartaric acid crystals, a source of cream of tartar. This baking powder is the fastest, which means you must bake your batter immediately. The only commercial tartrate baking powders I know of are Royal and Swansdown, and I can't find either of them in my local stores.

However, in her incredible collection of country lore, *Old Fashioned Recipe Book*, Carla Emery gives the following recipe for tartrate baking powder:*

"Mrs. Essemen's Baking Powder Recipe — Measure out 12.34 ounces (350 grams) of cream of tartar, 5.30 ounces (100 grams) bicarbonate of soda and 3.53 ounces (100 grams) of cornstarch. You don't actually have to be that precise, especially with the cornstarch, just even ounces will do. Sift them together ten times and spread them out to dry if there is any moisture in the batch.

"Generally the proportion of cream of tartar to soda should be 2 to 1. The cornstarch, remember, is only added to keep out the moisture and keep the ingredients from interacting with each other. If you decide to use this quick-action kind of baking powder remember to add your liquids at the end of your mixing order, and get the batter into the oven as quickly as possible. When using a recipe calling for double-acting baking powder, use about 1½ teaspoons to 2 teaspoons for each teaspoon called for in the recipe."

MASTER BAKING MIX

Here is a recipe for a biscuit-type mix which can be stored in the refrigerator for up to six weeks and substituted into any recipes calling for commercial biscuit mixes.

9 cups whole wheat pastry flour
⅓ cup baking powder   2½ teaspoons cream of tartar
4 teaspoons salt   2 cups soy shortening

*Reprinted with permission.

28

Stir baking powder, salt, and cream of tartar into flour. Sift together twice into large mixing bowl. Cut in shortening until mix is consistency of cornmeal. Store in tightly covered container.

THE MANY FORMS OF MILK

Milk is such a versatile food that we sometimes overlook its importance in our diet — it is just *there*. The U.S. Department of Agriculture Handbook No. 8, *Composition of Foods*, lists no less than sixteen line items under the milk category. Since there are so many different forms of milk, and so much confusion about their wholesomeness, I would like to define and discuss some of the more common ones.

The most basic form of milk is unpasteurized (raw) whole milk. While pasteurization was a timely and extremely valuable discovery, killing deadly bacteria in contaminated milk, modern microbiology has provided us with knowledge and techniques which make pasteurization unnecessary in many cases. Such a case would be with your own goat or cow, assuming that your milking techniques are impeccable and your animals are regularly innoculated and inspected against disease.

Another case is when a herd is under the close watch of a medical milk commission (such as regulates Certified Raw Milk) or a county health agency (such as in California regulates Guaranteed Raw Milk). Certified raw milk can be shipped anywhere within the state which accepts its certification; Guaranteed milk must be sold within the county which regulates its production. Both are heavily regulated and quite safe.

Many people are allergic to milk, and there is some evidence to indicate that some of those allergies can be avoided by the substitution of raw milk for pasteurized. Especially when the problem is a digestive one, often indicating a lactase deficiency (the enzyme, contained in raw milk, which aids to the breakdown of the milk protein), raw milk is tolerated better than pasteurized. A search for a safe source of raw milk is probably worth it if this is something you face.

When cream is removed from whole milk, the remaining liquid is described as "skimmed"; it may be low fat or nonfat, depending upon its butterfat content. Raw skimmed milk is available from some dairies. Raw cream is also available from some dairies, as is the resulting product, raw butter. Raw cheeses are also available.

Milk which has been pasteurized tends to be lower in calcium and certain antibodies and hormones, and the enzymes thought to be necessary for proper absorption of milk are destroyed. However, Vitamins A and D are usually added to commercially pasteurized milk, and if a safe source of raw milk is not available, pasteurized milk is certainly acceptable. Whole, skimmed, and other forms of milk are available in the pasteurized form.

Milk can be canned with modern pressure techniques. Evaporated (water partially removed) canned milk is a convenient, always available, form of milk, and I find it useful when making puddings, custards, and other items where the milk is to be heated anyway. Nutrients are lost in the heating of milk, and so canned milk should never be used as the primary form of milk in a household.

Powdered milk is available in several forms, and it is becoming more and more difficult to make an intelligent decision when purchasing it. There is powdered whole milk (available mostly in health food stores), noninstant nonfat milk, and two different types of instant nonfat milk — spray process and heat processed.

Previously, all instant powdered milk was made using a heat method which destroyed vitamins, minerals, enzymes and amino acids in addition to those which were destroyed in pasteurization. For this reason, health conscious writers (such as Adelle Davis) have traditionally recommended the use of noninstant powdered milk. Even today writers of books such as *Laurel's Kitchen* and *The Supermarket Handbook* have made this distinction.

Since the nutrient loss in dependent upon the heat used, however, when an instant powdered milk is made using the spray process it can be substituted for noninstant. How to tell? The only way I know is by the texture, since few manufacturers list "spray processed" on their packages. If the texture is fine and powdery, almost like flour, that is usually a spray process milk. If the milk is in granules, or crystals, it usually is the result of a heat process.

Yoghurt made with heat processed powdered milk tends to be stringy and lumpy; icings and gravies are gritty. In general, it is not acceptable for use in concentrated form in cooking.

Instant (or other heat-processed) milk powder can be added to milk-containing recipes or to a bottle of milk itself to fortify the resulting recipe, and instant milk works well in a blender when you are mixing beverages. I find uses for both kinds.

Adelle Davis, in *Let's Cook It Right*, cautions us not to rely upon powdered milk in any form as the main source of milk in a household, due to its nutritional weaknesses caused by heat. Nonfat milk in any form is a poor choice for the major milk source, especially of children, because it has a low fat content, and therefore limits the absorption of oil-soluble vitamins A and D. These vitamins contained in skim milk which is served at a meal containing fat is better absorbed than are the vitamins in skim milk served alone.

SUPERMILK

In a blender combine one quart whole raw or pasteurized milk, one cup instant or noninstant powdered milk, and one tablespoon protein powder (many types are available in health food stores). Blend at high speed for one or two minutes, then return to the bottle or carton. Use this milk on cereal, in puddings and custards, or anywhere else where a nutritional boost is desired.

SWEETENERS

We don't eat many sweetened foods at our house. Part of that is intentional — as we learned that sugar may be responsible for a number of ills we tried to reduce our consumption of it — and part of it is incidental to our busy lives. Desserts get forgotten. Sometimes *dinner* nearly gets forgotten, and so we try to put our energy to making sure that the time spent in the kitchen is well used.

However, sometimes we do make cookies, or coffee cakes, or puddings. I'm enough of a traditionalist to feel that tasty food is an integral part of celebration, whether that celebration be for a birthday, an anniversary or just for Sunday morning. So we do eat *some* sweetened foods. Ah — now I've admitted it. And how, some of you are asking, does she justify that? Does she shoot them so full of wheat germ and brewer's yeast that they are unpalatable, then feel smug when no one eats them?

Hardly. I'm proud to make chocolate chip cookies that my children want to share with their friends (although I use carob chips instead of chocolate, for reasons I covered in the carob section), and if I'm going to take the time to make brown rice pudding, I want to be able to enjoy it myself. So we do aim to make our treats tasty. However, we no longer use refined sugar, except to make syrup for the hummingbird feeder (honey has been known to transmit tongue fungus to hummers).

Refined white sugar, powdered or granulated, and brown sugar, even the stuff mislabeled "raw", are made from either sugar canes or sugar beets. The processes necessary to extract the final product are extensive, and the sugar industry goes to great lengths to produce a "pure" product. (Ironically, it is those very impurities which are removed during processing which provide the taste and nutrition in molasses, and which, had they been left in the sugar, would remove at least part of my argument against it.)

I find that as people begin to eat a more natural diet, their taste for sweet things diminishes gradually. As that begins to happen, they satisfy the craving for sweets (note — craving, not need) which they developed in their lollipop days by eating more complex carbohydrates like brown rice, whole grain bread, and peanut butter, and natural sweets such as apples, oranges, apricots, and dates.

A common progression is to move from white sugar to brown sugar, gradually reducing the amount of either. A jar of honey or a bowl of crystallized dates may replace the sugar bowl after a while, and on Sunday mornings, molassess, sorghum and real maple syrup will often have more takers than the 2% maple syrup that has been used for years.

Many families find that after a few years they lose the sugar canister in the back of a cupboard, and discover when they need Karo syrup in a recipe Aunt Myrtle gave them that they ran out of it months ago and didn't notice.

When I am baking bread, I use honey, molasses, sorghum or maple syrup interchangeably. When I bake sweets such as cookies, puddings, cakes or souffles, I lean more toward the lighter honeys such as clover or sage unless the flavor of darker honey is desirable, such as in gingersnaps. I, too, have made the progression from white sugar to honey in much the way I described above, and some of you who have my earlier recipes, such as the ones in *The Book of Whole Grains*, know that I once used brown sugar freely in baking. I still do occasionally, but most of the time I stick to the other sweeteners.

HONEY

Honey can be used to replace white sugar in almost all of its uses. If you must sweeten your tea, use honey; if you are canning fruit or making jam, use honey; gelatin desserts can be made from pure fruit juices, usually without flavor assistance, but if they are tart, use honey.

Honey has a lot going for it — it is sweeter than sugar, it can be produced on your own property without complicated refining equipment, it is easier on the body, and it even contains small quantities of nutrients. HOWEVER, it must be remembered when you switch to honey that it still makes people fat, and it still causes cavities. Honey treats are just as bad for children's teeth (some dentists say worse) and should not be a regular indulgence.

33

How do you make the switch? A good guideline at first is to substitute ¾ cup honey for each cup of sugar called for in a recipe, and to decrease the liquid by l/4 cup. If there is no liquid, you will have to add a little flour, from two tablespoons to ¼ cup for each cup of honey.

If your recipe calls for brown sugar, use half molasses and half honey in the same proportion as above, or use this suggestion from *Supermarket Handbook*, by Nikki and David Goldbeck:

> "...retain ¼ to ½ the sugar (use "raw" sugar) and let the rest of the measure be molasses. For each cup of molasses you include add ½ teaspoon of baking soda (to neutralize the acidity) and omit the baking powder. For each cup of molasses reduce the liquid in the recipe by ¼ cup."

BLACKSTRAP AND MOLASSES

Blackstrap molasses is one of the classic "health foods". When someone is maligning "those health food faddists", blackstrap is often pointed out as an example of the unlikely foods the so-called faddists insist upon eating, along with their alfalfa sprouts, their wheat germ, and their brewer's yeast.

I can see why. One booklet, written by Cyril Scott (*Crude Black Molasses, The Natural Wonder-Food*), gives examples of blackstrap cures for arthritis, strokes, ulcers, eczema, high blood pressure, colitis, varicose veins, cancer, and mental dullness. This type of propaganda tends to mask the real values and uses of a food (or any product, for that matter).

Searching through books for references to blackstrap, I found that Rombauer and Becker (*Joy of Cooking*) dismiss it is unpalatable, Dickens (*Nicolas Nickleby*) immortalized it as "brimstone and treacle", *Housekeeping in Old Virginia* (1879) ignored it, and several health food cookbooks call for it in their recipes without telling you what it is, what it does for you, or where you can get it.

So I think it's time someone gave blackstrap a reasonable hearing. Blackstrap is not strictly a "natural" food — any more than are wheat germ or bran. Those two healthful items are natural enough when left on the grain of wheat and ground into whole wheat flour, but it could be argued that when they are sifted out from the flour and eaten separately, they constitute a less natural product. In the same sense, blackstrap, and in fact all molasses, is merely the byproduct of a sugar refining process, and not natural at all.

Crystalline white sugar is created by pressing sugar cane or sugar beets through massive rollers and refining the resulting juice by the use of heat and chemicals (the most commonly used seem to be lime, carbon dioxide and sulfur dioxide, although hundreds of different ones have been used). Most kinds of molasses are the result of this process, and contain numerous dissolved gases and chemicals, probably the least desirable of which is sulfur.

Unsulfured molasses is a deliberately manufactured product; thus its higher price. It is pressed from cane and precipitated out of the juice without the use of sulfur, and results in a syrup which is vastly preferable in taste and healthfulness.

Blackstrap is the so-called "waste product" of all this. It is a result of the third and final boiling, during which just about all of the water and sugar are removed from the juice, allowing most of the sucrose to separate from the solution and crystallize. Blackstrap can of course be made from the same process that produces unsulfured molasses, being then unsulfured blackstrap.

It is illuminating to study the Department of Agriculture's booklet, *Nutritive Values of Foods* (USDA Home and Garden Bulletin No. 7s, revised April 1977). One tablespoon of blackstrap is listed as containing 137 milligrams of calcium, 17 milligrams of phosphorus, 3.2 milligrams of iron, and 585 milligrams of potassium (that's more potassium than most people get in a whole day — my high-powered multiple vitamin capsule only contains 30 milligrams).

Granulated white sugar contains no measurable vitamins or minerals. Even brown sugar, which is merely white sugar with a little molasses added back in, contains only 12 milligrams of calcium, 3 milligrams of phosphorus, 47.3 milligrams of potassium and .5 milligrams of iron.

You can make your own brown sugar, and a richer one than you can find in the store, by blending blackstrap molasses with white sugar. Start by stirring a tablespoon of molasses into a cup of sugar, blend thoroughly, then add dribbles more until the right consistency is reached. Because blackstrap molasses contains far more iron and calcium than other types of molasses, the brown sugar made with it will carry a little nutrition along with the sweetness, although the flavor may take a little getting used to. If it doesn't go over well, use regular light or dark molasses.

So what does all this mean? I do not mean to imply that you should start downing blackstrap molasses each morning as a vitamin supplement (unless you feel that's the only way you will get enough potassium and iron), nor do I make any claims for blackstrap's healing abilities.

However, molasses is an alternative to sugar which has a lot of merits, and blackstrap is far superior nutritionally to ordinary molasses. It also contains less residue sugar. Blackstrap, therefore, is not so sweet as sugar, so you may want to add it half and half with honey for some uses. If you do substitute one of these less empty, liquid sweeteners into a recipe, cut the liquid down about 1/4 cup for each cup used.

SORGHUM AND MAPLE SYRUP

There's a story that says Benjamin Franklin found a seed or three still attached to the straw of an imported broom, planted it, and thus started the sorghum industry in America. That's probably stretching the truth a bit, but he might well have been responsible for popularizing this strange plant in the U.S., where it was not grown at the time.

Fields of sorghum look like fields of corn, and many people drive past them without realizing they are seeing acres of the grain which feeds millions of people in Africa, China, and Japan. In this country we usually feed it to pigs.

There are several varieties of sorghum, and most of them are not grown for their grain at all, but for their stalks. *Sorgos*, or syrup sorghums, are primarily grown for the syrup which can be extracted from their stalks, and which makes an excellent substitute for artificial maple syrup on pancakes. (Did you know that what we call maple syrup generally has less than 5% pure maple syrup in it? Some has none. Read the label.)

Comparing the nutritional contents of maple syrup, sorghum, and honey, it seems that in many ways sorghum is superior to maple syrup (more calcium, phosphorus and iron), although the potassium content is much higher in maple syrup, and sorghum is higher in several vitamins and minerals than uncooked honey, although the honey contains many more trace elements than either sorghum or maple syrup. Corn syrup, by the way, the major ingredient of most commercial pancake syrups, is considerably lower in all nutrients and higher in both calories and carbohydrates than any of the other three.

When you buy sorghum or maple syrup, check the label to make certain that you are getting the real thing. I accidentally purchased a three-pound tin labeled "pure sorghum syrup" which on closer inspection read "Ingredients: corn syrup and pure sorghum". I still don't know how much sorghum there is in that syrup, but since it is the second ingredient, it's for sure less than half.

Maple trees are harvested primarily in the U.S. and Canadian northeast, and the price of maple syrup is higher the further west you travel. If you have an opportunity to stock up on this precious commodity during family vacations or business trips, do so — its high sugar content helps it to keep for quite a long time (although we refrigerate ours to extend that period).

Try sorghum or maple syrup in your baked goods as well as on your pancakes and waffles. Warmed slightly before use (a good trick with honey also), it thins out and pours more easily. If you substitute it in recipes calling for honey, use it one to one. If you want to use it in recipes calling for refined sugar, reduce the liquids in the recipe by about one-fourth the amount of sorghum you are using, and use ¾ cup of sorghum for each cup of sugar called for.

Here is a use for either syrup which is a tasty addition to fresh fruit, puddings, or breakfast cereal.

SWEET YOGHURT SAUCE

1 cup plain whole milk yoghurt
⅓ cup sorghum or maple syrup
½ teaspoon ground cinnamon

Cream yoghurt and syrup together (it helps to warm the syrup slightly first). Stir in cinnamon and serve.

HIDDEN SUGAR

On a scale of one to ten as a measurement of my annoyance, added sugars have usually only worked me up to four or five, because I'm well aware that most people who buy whipping cream, or pectin, or ascorbic acid for fruit, will then add sugar to their preparation. And those of us who are trying to reduce our intake of sugar are fairly aware of its inclusion in such products, and will purchase others.

But potato chips? Peanut butter? SALT? Ever since Gloria Swanson announced the message of William Dufty's *Sugar Blues* on national television, sincerely concerned consumers have been trying to cut down on their dietary uses of sugar. It doesn't seem fair to me that they cannot even trust a package of potato chips, yet that is the latest place I found sugar hidden.

In an unfamiliar market recently, trying to find a snack to hold me over until dinner, I succumbed to a sign which said "country style potato chips". The front of the label loudly proclaimed "NO PRESERVA-TIVES; NO ARTIFICIAL INGREDIENTS". The back of the label, however, contained the following list: reconstituted dehydrated potatoes (that's NATURAL?), salt, sugar, dextrose. Sugar? Dextrose? Why?

And recently (I must have been the last one to hear) one of the children in my cooking class told me that Skippy peanut butter contains sugar. I'd only seen the old-fashioned type of this particular brand, and so had to go to the store to check it out for myself. Sure enough — sugar in peanut butter.

But the hidden ingredient which sent my ire up to 9.9 was the sugar in a package of plain, ordinary salt. What can sugar possibly do to improve salt? As a matter of fact, it is added to improve flow, but just the same, salt is eaten in far too large a quantity in this country as it is, and so is sugar — why compound the problem? Trying to buy a package of salt in a hurry one night, no natural food stores nearby, I was unable in that particular supermarket to find a package of salt which did not contain sugar.

Were you aware that these three items contained sugar? I feel very strongly that we should always read labels when considering a new product, but just the same, putting sugar in food which one doesn't normally consider to be a sugar-spiked item seems to be dishonest. Isn't this what would once have been called adulteration?

Purchasing food in supermarkets requires time (to read the labels), patience (to keep putting items back on the shelf and trying new ones), and a sense of humor (when after an hour of shopping you only have six items in your grocery cart).

The whole experience reminds me of an anecdote Dufty (*Sugar Blues*) tells of a cross-country drive. Reading the menu at a roadside restaurant in search of something without sugar, he despaired of finding anything at all to eat. "Breads, rolls, pastries, crackers and cookies, donuts and waffles," he writes, "pancakes and toast, jellies and jam, relish and ketchup, vegetables and fruit, meat and potatoes, soup to nuts, everything is frozen, prepared, pepped up with sugar."

He rejects baked beans and sugar-cured bacon, oatmeal salted with sugar-spiked salt, and finally settles for clam chowder, which "like everything else, reminds you how good clam chowder used to be in some long ago lost time." As he pays his bill and prepares to leave, Dufty picks up a can of clam chowder displayed by the register for customers to take home and cook themselves. The first ingredient listed is sugar — more sugar, as he points out, than clams!

It's time for us to speak out — and we can do that by refusing to buy foods which have sugar slipped into their formulas. How can we

help our bodies to rid themselves of their addiction-like craving for sugar unless we know where they are getting it?

Read the labels, make your decision, then announce your reason to the manager of your regular grocery store. Tell him that the reason you no longer buy lemon pepper, or a certain brand of boullion cubes, or canned tomato soup, is because there is sugar added and you don't feel it should be. Ask him to check other brands of the same items — educate him to your needs.

Sugar intake should be something we each can regulate, but we must know where the sugar is coming from in order to reduce it in our diets.

JEAN McMANIS

EATING SMALL

BREASTFED IS BEST FED

One of the similarities I have noticed about the mothers who attend my natural foods cooking classes is that many of them have breastfed one or more of their children. It makes sense. As we become more concerned about eating the most natural forms of food, it seems logical that we would want to give our children the same benefits we seek. Starting infants on breast milk instead of on pasteurized, sterilized, chemically fortified and sugar-sweetened formula is a reasonable extension of that logic.

A few years ago I attended a symposium on infant feeding practices. One of the speakers, Derrick B. Jelliffe, M.D., spoke about the biological specificity of milk. What that means, in plain terms, is that rat milk is good for rats, goat milk is great for goats, and human milk is perfect for human beings. Cow milk is perfectly suited for growing healthy baby cows, but it is not so perfect for growing baby humans.

Chemical and physical differences in the composition of cows' milk, goats' milk, and human milk make them quite unique, and unsuitable for random exchange between species.

The iron and protein contents of milk are good examples. The actual measurable amounts of iron contained in samples of cows' milk and human milk are similar. Because the iron contained in breast milk is 49% absorbed, however, and all of that is utilized, while that in cows' milk is poorly assimilated, the iron content in breast milk is more adequate for the baby's good health.

According to Frederick Lloyd, M.D., of Stanford University Department of Pediatrics, totally breastfed infants rarely develop iron deficiency anemia. Babies who are fed ordinary or iron-fortified cows' milk formula have an extremely low rate of iron absorption, and also tend to become constipated from the large amount of undigested material in their stools.

Cows' milk protein is also difficult for babies to digest, and cows' milk contains a different proportion of amino acids, the components of protein, than does breast milk. Since the hard curds which form in a child's stomach from cows' milk formulas often cause a feeling of fullness, the baby may go longer between meals. Also, since the milk cannot be fed undiluted without severe discomfort, the diluted form in which it is given requires that the baby drink more and work harder to absorb the necessary nutrients.

41

This whole absorption problem occurs with other components of milk, and effectively guarantees that merely comparing nutrient amounts, then matching and adjusting them chemically will *not* provide an adequate substitute for the natural product. We do not know how the body regulates the absorption of vitamins, minerals, proteins, carbohydrates, and fats, but we do know that when they are fed breast milk, nearly all babies thrive. When fed substitute formulas, many babies develop subtle nutritional deficiencies, gastric disturbances, and even allergies, and are much more susceptible to upper respiratory infections.

There are many wonderful arguments for breastfeeding besides the nutritional ones, including protection against allergies and disease in the early months, and psychological relationships between mothers and their children. There isn't room to expand on them here, but we recommend anyone interested in learning more seek books on the subject. Two excellent volumes are *The Womanly Art of Breastfeeding*, by La Leche League International, and *Breastfeeding Your Baby*, by Karen Pryor.

These books also include valuable advice about handling the mechanics of breastfeeding in a nonsupportive culture, mechanics which can really get in the way of the important stuff if they are allowed to. Dr. Jelliffe discussed this problem at the Symposium, and in a paper published in the *Boston Medical and Surgical Journal* ("Current Concepts in Nutrition; Breast is Best", Vol. 297, No. 17, October 27, 1977).

In his paper, Dr. Jelliffe included a diagram labeled "The Anxiety-Nursing Failure Syndrome", which clearly showed the damage that can be done to a mother's first attempts to breastfeed her infant by anxiety, uncertainty, sore nipples, breast engorgement and other similar difficulties. (I might add that nonsupportive aunts, critical neighbors, and uncertain husbands don't help much, either.)

Jellife's recommendation for dealing with these mechanics (and the resulting emotional difficulties) is the formation of mother peer groups to boost morale and disseminate information. Local chapters of La Leche League International serve exactly this purpose, and can offer a great deal of support to the new mother. It was at a La Leche League meeting that I met the woman who eventually taught me about natural foods and vegetarianism, and many of the women who have influenced, reflected, and helped to develop my thinking about living with and nurturing children.

No special diet is required of the nursing mother, but if you are pregnant OR nursing your nutrition should be more than ordinarily complete. Any weaknesses in your diet, according to findings in

42

malnourished Third World areas, will show in your health before it will in your baby's.

So eat especially well during your pregnancy — make every calorie count. Calcium, iron, vitamins A, D, E, B and C — all will be present in the milk to as great a degree as the mother's body can provide them, and if there are not sufficient reserves to leave enough for mother's health, then that is what suffers. Obviously, if the nutrition of the mother is *very* poor (such as when she is living on potato chips and cola), the nutritional content of the milk will also begin to suffer, according to Dr. Jelliffe, as well as the quantity of it.

Most babies, if healthy at birth and receiving breast milk from a healthy mother, need no supplementary juice, water, solids or vitamin supplements until the age of five or six months. Vitamins and early solid feedings are often necessary for artificially fed babies; the natural milk supply contains everything babies need for that first half year, and good nutrition combined with chopped up "people food" for the rest of their babyhood.

As pediatricians and obstetricians relearn the facts about breast-feeding, more mothers-to-be will be able to find supportive and informed professionals to help them learn about infant nutrition. Until then, read what you can, contact a local breastfeeding support group such as La Leche League, and rely on your own good sense to know that natural food is best for babies, just like it is for grownups.

TEETHING TREATS FOR TODDLERS

Since most babies get twenty teeth in their first three years, it's not difficult to understand why discomfort and crankiness are common symptoms in a toddler. Most babies experience only occasional pain from teething, just before a tooth breaks the gum, but all teethers are unhappy some of the time.

Since most American homes now have freezers, or at least freezer compartments of refrigerators, the following tasty snacks should be easy to provide for your child during his teething days. A few minutes spent preparing these and storing them will save whole afternoons of trying to deal with an unhappy baby. Adults think of cold foods as being refreshing in the heat, but less so in the midst of winter, but teething children seem to like popsicles as much in December as June.

When tooth misery reaches its greatest, many children refuse to nurse or eat. Try some of these foods at mealtime, and see if they are more readily accepted than warm dishes.

FROZEN FRUIT

The easiest teething food to prepare is frozen fruit. The best fruits for this are ripe but firm bananas, peaches, nectarines, melons, and pears. Wash and peel the fruit, then cut into sizes that a baby can handle. Slice bananas into four vertical slices. Wrap pieces of fruit in waxed paper or plastic wrap. Roll from the edge of the paper inwards, adding pieces as the previous ones are covered by the paper so that no two pieces of fruit touch (they will stick together if they do).

REFRIGERATED FRUIT

I've never tried to freeze watery fruits such as plums, tomatoes, apples, or figs, but they keep nicely in the refrigerator, and feel good on sore gums, from the response of teethers. All of them except apples are messy to eat, so they are best kept for high chair eating. Cold wedges of peeled apple are usually accepted happily by a fussy teether, even before the first tooth appears, but watch for too-large chunks disappearing into the inexperienced mouth, which happens after the apple gets a bit worn.

SHERBETS AND ICES

With a little enthusiasm on your part, many tasty treats can be made from fruits with a high water content (melons are great for this), placed in plastic ice-cube trays (the ones that have separate divisions for each cube), with popsicle sticks inserted. Search popular magazines and books for a range of recipes, but basically the principle is to remove seeds and skin, mash or puree in a blender, and freeze. Fruit juices may be frozen; so may some custards and gelatin desserts, but avoid using honey in anything you make for children under one year. Botulism spores have been found in some honey samples which can be harmful to babies, so if sweetening is really necessary, it would be safer to use apple juice or even sugar.

MEATS AND VEGETABLES

One of the easiest meats to freeze for your child is the good old American hot dog. Buy coloring- and nitrate-free wieners from the freezer section of your supermarket or natural food store, then wrap them individually in waxed paper or plastic wrap, making certain that the paper surrounds each wiener entirely and that no two are touching each other. To serve, unwrap the paper until you come to the first one; remove, and reroll the others and return to the freezer.

Other meats may be frozen, also. Strips of cooked chicken, liver, heart, kidney — judge the appropriateness of the meat by its fiber content. Will it be stringy as it thaws? Then avoid it until your child is chewing meat at his or her meals.

Some vegetables, notably carrots and string beans, lend themselves very nicely to freezing after cooking. Use the same waxed paper rolling technique to store them, and serve them one at a time.

TRICKS AND TREATS

— FEEDING FUSSY KIDS

Sometimes even the most cheerful and cooperative children stop eating for a while, usually after a growth spurt or a bout of illness. My usual tendency is to wait it out and bite my tongue before issuing the second "Aren't you going to eat any more?" of the meal. When they aren't hungry, children tend to be more choosy (aren't adults?), and turning meal times into power struggles may result in hurt feelings at the least, and more permanent food avoidances at the worst. So don't push too hard.

However, if specific food avoidances crop up anyway, rather than forcing the issue you can sometimes use drama and pleasantries to work them through. For example, when my children after a lengthy duel with the common cold started leaving the room as soon as I suggested "How about some more juice?", I bought a pair of trick vinyl straws, the kind that are tied in knots. The requests for juice tripled for the next three days. Inexpensive cups with built-in straws had the same effect this cold season.

I used to make faces in my two-year old's oatmeal, using dried apple slices cut in half for eyebrows, corn nuts for eyes, an almond for a nose, and raisins for a smiling mouth. Flake coconut formed messy hair, and John's smiling eyes and cheerful eating were my reward. (Hot cereal was often refused by my son, otherwise known as the "grape nuts kid".)

Pizzas made from tortillas — celery stick people with cherry tomato noses and sliced olive eyes held on by toothpicks (leaves stay on to form hair) — soup served in a special-occasion bowl with a picture on the bottom which appears as the soup disappears — these are tricks to make it more attractive for children to eat the food you, with your judgment, have chosen to serve.

"Eat your peas or no dessert" might escape each of our lips once in a while, but we all know that it's not the best way. Trying to make good food attractive and fun, not all the time but once in a while, is more effective.

FORMING LIFETIME EATING STYLES

How vividly I remember being required to sit at the dinner table with my mother and father, my aunt and uncle, my grandmother and my grandfather, when I was six years old. It was summer and I just HAD to get back outside and finish building that fort. There were only two of us children in that severely over-adulted home, and we nightly suffered through the requisite lectures on table manners and cleanliness and children-starving-in-India in squirmy silence, eating as little as we could get away with and slipping outside again as soon as we were released.

I still have the "finish what's on your plate" syndrome, making it very difficult for me to eat a reasonable, rather than a gluttonous, portion when I eat out, and my appetite is often regulated by the clock rather than by my internal needs. I wonder how much my continual weight problem is due to those early sessions at the family meal table.

Small children are notoriously fidgety eaters, and mine are no different. Like me when I was six, they don't want to sit still long enough to get a decent meal. Having found that attempts to make them remain through an entire mealtime usually resulted in bad tempers and food on the floor, and not in an increased intake of food, my tendency has typically been to try to slip a good breakfast into each of them before they awaken enough to discover what has been done to them, and then hope for the best for the rest of the day.

But THAT didn't even work when summer arrived, and they were jumping out of bed, fully awake, at daybreak, and heading for the sandbox before I even made it to the kitchen. Suddenly I realized that it seemed a bit unrealistic to expect infants who had been fed on demand to become three-meal-a-day people by the time they were three or four years old.

Why not continue to feed the child on demand in much the same way as we had the infant? Might it not contribute to a closer response to the actual hunger needs instead of developing an eight, twelve and five o'clock hunger?

Carrying this thought a little further, if we didn't think in terms of three meals a day and snacks in between, but simply in terms of an overall intake of food, it would be easier to plan a day's "meals", put them into several plastic refrigerator containers each morning, and reach into them several times a day to satisfy the active children's hunger as it occurred.

I have been trying that ever since, and feel that it is a great success. In the morning I slice carrots, celery, turnips, apple, or cucumbers in some combination and place them in one plastic box. In another I put a few handfuls of raisins, almonds, cashews, chip coconut, sunflower seeds, and toasted soybeans from a large jar which we keep in the kitchen. I make a sandwich and divide it into fourths, or cut up leftover chicken or roast into small pieces. In one plastic container goes a small portion of cooked vegetables (usually leftovers from the night before); in another, a few home made cookies, or crackers and cheese. All of this takes less than half an hour.

The children still sit with us for meals, but that's mostly a social thing. It's a time when we can be together for a few minutes to talk about the bee which frightened Doña Ana from her swing set, or the shadow which John discovered following him around, and at the end of the day it is a welcome opportunity for Dad to see his children. But if after five or ten minutes they get twitchy, and begin to move the food around on their plates, we can let them disappear back to the sandbox or the tinkertoys without fretting, because we know they've eaten fairly well earlier in the day.

Children who tend to avoid vegetables at meals will sometimes devour raw vegetables when they are served as finger food while they are playing outside. All children (and most adults) tire of the same ordinary vegetables. Try serving different ones — cauliflower, zucchini, jicama, broccoli, bell pepper, mushrooms. (As an aside, think about ways to slip vegetables into regular meals in an unexpected form. When chopped or grated very fine, many vegetables which children wouldn't ordinarily eat alone can be incorporated into another dish, for example, a souffle or a quiche.)

Leftover vegetables from our snack bowl go into soups, casseroles, tuna salads, etc., for a future meal. Grated carrot and finely chopped celery, for example, enliven tuna or chicken sandwiches. Sliced vegetables color yesterday's reheated soup or tossed salad.

One of the most obvious benefits of this new way of feeding our little ones has been the reduction in undesirable snacks — potato chips, candies, cookies — which used to be requested several times a day and which I would sometimes let them have just out of tiredness and frustration. When I neglect to provide them with adequate variety and substance even now, the requests for gum, or candy, or potato chips, return — and send me back to my chopping board!

I have found that I also tend to snack from the children's containers rather than rummaging around for something more caloric, and the extra time it takes in the morning to prepare the correct amount of food in the plastic boxes is more than worthwhile for the effect it has had on my waistline.

It seems to me that we might all benefit from the snacking (on good food) way of eating. Mealtimes are, after all, a social as well as a nutritional exercise. There are ways to prolong a mealtime without eating very much, such as designing make-it-yourself salads, or tacos, or sandwiches, and in the time it takes each of you to make your own salad, for example, you probably could have eaten two helpings of lasagne.

JEAN McMANIS

EATING NATURALLY
ON A TRIP

This snack trick works well at home, but how about when you're away? I packed lunchboxes for my preschoolers when we would be away from home more than an hour, and they served themselves of these same foods, in addition to a thermos half filled with water or juice. If the trip was a long one, there would be lunchboxes for midday, and a sack full of fruit and nuts, for snacks. No longer did we stop at McDonalds after a shopping trip, or return home with hysterical children who were not only tired, but also ravenous.

Trips to other people's home can be a problem, too, if a meal is not planned during your stay. Rather than hint to my hostess to fix my children something to eat when they start to kick the dog or pick fights (such hints are definitely not Emily Post approved), I just take out my bag of snack mix and pass it around to everyone in sight. Amazing how it helps.

ON THE ROAD

When we are driving a long distance, an ice chest is a must. Traveling with children involves so many stops anyway, to see the rocks, to gather leaves, to find a bathroom. Who needs to stop at Hamburger Heaven as well? Even staying in motels you can take much of your food along. A quart of milk purchased at night will serve very nicely in the morning to moisten granola or muesli, and several pieces of fresh fruit combined with the ever-present mix of nuts and seeds and raisins, and you're all set to climb the Empire State Building or walk across Golden Gate Bridge.

I try to avoid restaurant breakfasts, since so often the omelets are made from powdered eggs, the juices are sweetened and insipid, and the sausages, bacon, and ham are cured with nitrates and inevitably greasy. There are exceptions, of course. I found a coffee shop chain in Los Angeles which squeezes the orange juice within sight of your table, brings slices of bread (whole wheat is available) to your table for toasting, and offers several whole grain cereal and egg dishes made with fresh eggs. That kind of place is definitely to be encouraged, so I make a point of eating there whenever I'm in town. On the whole, though, we prepare our own breakfasts in our car or motel room.

Lunches and dinners depend upon where we are. If it's feasible, we'll visit a natural food store, buy some groceries, and picnic in the park. We've done that, even in Washington D.C. A natural foods restaurant shows up once in a while, and we'll splurge and eat out if we find one. On the whole, the restaurants which we can afford do not serve food we are willing to eat, and we try to avoid going into them. Once or twice a week we will have a meal in a place we couldn't afford to visit every night, but most of the time we make do with grocery stores, natural food stores, picnics, and meals in motel rooms.

IN THE CAMPGROUND

When we go camping it gets easier. Usually. One summer we were camping in the desert. We ate fairly well the first few days, living off the supplies we had brought from home. Eventually we ran out of milk and eggs, and fruits and vegetables, and we thought it would be nice to get something to add variety to the nuts and raisins and cheese and bread that we had been eating each day for lunch.

So we climbed into the car and drove to the nearest town. As we entered the grocery store, I knew we were going to have problems. The first aisle was filled with the really essential items for the camper — suntan lotion, shampoo, aspirin, flashlight batteries, and insect repellent. The next aisle consisted of girlie magazines, beer, soft drinks, marsh mallows, and potato chips.

You've all seen the type of store I was faced with. They struggle with expensive trucking rates and sporadic sales curves, and try valiantly to keep in stock all the emergency items the campers forgot or run out of, or break. And they try to keep everybody happy — the smoker, the drinker, the teenagers, the children, the retired couple. But they don't yet know about people like us. There was no whole wheat flour, no yoghurt without artificial coloring and sugar, no breakfast cereal without preservatives, no real maple syrup or raw honey, no whole wheat bread.

What do you do in a situation like this? You're going to be in it next summer, unless you take your vacation in Santa Cruz, or Berkeley, or somewhere similar. Lake Tahoe, Yosemite, Mount Rushmore, Yellow stone, the Pocanos — they aren't ready for natural foods in the campgrounds yet. So what can you do to make it for two weeks or so in the wilderness of ordinary vacation grocery stores? I have a few suggestions.

CARRY SOME STAPLES. Take powdered milk, wheat germ, brewer's yeast, carob powder, whole wheat flour, brown rice, dried beans and several kinds of nuts. They fit nicely in coffee cans or plastic boxes. If you wind up buying a pancake mix because you just aren't up to making pancakes from scratch in camp, fortify the mix with wheat germ and powdered milk before you add water. Stir powdered milk into the pasteurized milk you buy. Use carob powder to flavor milk

instead of buying soft drinks; keep bottles of fruit juice on ice. Brown rice can be soaked in boiling water at breakfast time when the stove is lit, and it takes less cooking time in the evening (same with beans).

BUY NEUTRAL ITEMS. If you cannot buy healthy food, at least avoid buying unhealthy food. Instead of soft drinks, buy a sixpack of canned fruit juices, or even juice drinks. Try to avoid chemical additives, though, even if you have to accept sugar. If you can't buy maple syrup, buy honey rather than artificially flavored sugar syrup. If you can't buy fruit-flavored yoghurt without coloring or sugar, buy plain yoghurt and add fresh fruit and honey.

EAT LOTS OF PROTEIN, THEN FILL IN WITH FRUIT AND VEGETABLES. When you are getting strenuous exercise, which you probably are while camping, you need lots of protein. Get that from nuts and seeds, and from the cheese and eggs you buy at the grocery. Meat does not keep well in camp, so plan to eat less of that. Take a copy of *Diet For A Small Planet* (Frances Moore Lappe) with you to help you complement your proteins.

Fruits and vegetable can be kept in string bags in camp, or in the ice chest for several days. Eat them raw if it's too hot to cook — don't succumb to potato chips and soft drinks for the duration of your trip, or you will find that you return from your vacation with less energy than you had when you left home.

ON THE TRAIL

I recently met someone who spent two months hiking in the mountains. Among other things, we spoke about his emergence into civilization after two months in near solitude. I vividly remember bursting with desire for a hot shower and a hamburger after only four days of backpacking a few years ago, and while my new friend agreed that the hot shower he treated himself to each time he hit the pavement was a real treat, he had none of my cravings for "civilized" food. Recalling the tastelessness of freeze-dried hiking food, I asked him how he had survived for two months (not to mention how he had been able to afford over one hundred meals at mountaineering store prices) on such fare without developing food cravings.

His answer was so simple it surprised me. He hadn't purchased any prepared hiking food at all, but had made all his own meals from dehydrated fruits and vegetables prepared at home the previous summer, combined with nuts, beans and seeds ground or chopped in a blender for faster cooking. He had come down from the mountains four or five times to replenish his supplies, picking up a few fresh fruits and vegetables to add variety, and consequently he ate as well, if not better, as he did at home.

It would take a bit of practice at home before I would risk taking off for several days limited by home-prepared meals such as he described, but I think it would be fun to try. He said he had developed all of his recipes from meals he usually cooked in one pot or baked in a casserole, then put beans, brown rice, whole barley, dried corn, lentils, etc., into his blender at a high speed for a second or two just to chop them into smaller pieces.

You could use a flour mill set to the coarsest grind the same way. Combining half a cup of brown rice grits, for example, with dehydrated onions, parsley, chile powder, garlic salt, dehydrated tomatoes, and other seasonings would give you a kind of spanish rice mix — when the time came to cook it, you would pour the contents from the plastic bag into a pot, add about two cups of water, bring to a boil and simmer slowly for about fifteen minutes, until tender.

The same sort of thing can be done with split pea or lentil soup; crack the peas into small pieces and combine in a bag with powdered milk, dehydrated onions, perhaps some jerky, salt and herbs, and you have your own instant soup mix. There are some excellent natural soup bases available now in natural food stores — beef, chicken, carrot, parsley, onion, and a variety of mixed vegetable flavors — which contain far less salt than boullion cubes, and no preservatives or monosodium glutamate. The one I have seen most often is made by Vigor Cup, of Bellmore, New York, but there are others.

54

Adding a teaspoon of these soup bases to a bag containing whole wheat or vegetable macaroni, dehydrated vegetables, grated parmesan cheese and herbs or spices provides you with a macaroni casserole. The possibilities are limitless. The Sierra Club publishes an excellent book which may serve to help you get started preparing your own camping fare. *Natural Foods For the Pack*, written by Vikki Kinmont, has dozens of tasty recipes and some good ideas to build from.

It is even possible to purchase prepared natural food meals in packages which make two or three servings each. Two brands are relatively well-represented in natural foods stores, or they can be obtained directly from the manufacturer.

Natural Food Backpack Dinners (P.O. Box 532, Corvallis, Oregon 97330) have meals such as Country Corn Chowder, Mountain Macaroni, Meadow Mushroom Soup, and Hearty Lentil Soup. I often use their Vegetable Minestrone for dinner — one package will feed myself and my two children, with leftovers for lunch; it is an excellent rich-tasting minestrone.

The other organization, Earthwonder, Inc., makes Natural Meals-in-a-Box, with titles such as Fruit & Nut Rice, Mushroom-Wheat Pilaf, Millet Stew, Spanish Rice and Curry Rice. Their address is Earthwonder Farm, Blue Eye, Missouri 65611. The Natural Food Backpack Dinners cook in 15 to 20 minutes; Natural Meals-in-a-Box take somewhat longer, as the grains have been left in their whole form in most cases.

Breastfed babies fare best of all on the trail. A lot of extra fluid for the nursing mother, of course, and put in some clean finger foods, such as crackers, dried fruit or apples for the older toddler (bananas are OUT while Junior is being carried on someone's back — besides, they don't fare well in the pack).

Whole grain cereals, ground finely, and applesauce made from freeze-dried fruit granules, available at food storage-oriented natural food stores, will appease nearly all children's palates in the fresh air mornings. During the rest of the day, fortified a little more often with snacks, they can eat the same food as the grownups.

EATING THROUGH THE DAY

HEALTHY BREAKFASTS

Have you ever read the side panel of a box of breakfast cereal? Ever wondered just how they make Krispie Krinkles or Shrunken Wheat Wonders? Of course you've never been guilty of skipping breakfast, or of letting your children do so, right? And I don't suppose anyone in your house has ever eaten leftover cheesecake for breakfast?

Well, if you can say no to all of these questions, you are way ahead of me! Because I have read the side panel of many breakfast cereals, and I've wondered sufficiently about the production methods of them to tour a cornflake factory; the information gleaned from those two activities makes me furious. And yet at the same time the breakfast situation in our house has wandered around from medium good to awful for years, and that frustrates me.

First of all, I'm not necessarily saying the old-fashioned way was better. Eggs, bacon, hot biscuits with fresh butter and piles of flapjacks with real maple syrup may have been filling and nutritious, but they were also highly caloric and full of cholesterol. Weren't they? And they are hardly appropriate for today's sedentary desk-worker. Are they?

But they did help people make it from dawn to noon without dizzy spells, growling stomachs, and midmorning grouches. And children who went off to play after such hearty meals generally left the kitchen happily and often were busy with their exploring and learning for hours, not being heard of again until noon.

Television commercials notwithstanding, I just cannot imagine Huckleberry Finn starting off on his travels after a breakfast of ChocoBalls and OranguTang, can you? Even cornflakes and grape juice drink would have left him with a case of the hungries before he made it far from shore.

In our own miniature laboratory (my kitchen), my two experimental subjects (Doña Ana and John) have proved over and over that when I get lazy and succumb to their pleas for packaged cereal or a leftover cupcake for breakfast, we have a higher rate of tantrums (theirs) and increased incidents of headaches (mine) before noon than when I wash my face with cold water, boil some eggs or steam some whole grain cereal and feed them (and me) properly.

We visited a cornflake factory once. Dried kernels of corn, nutritious at the outset, were soaked in a lye bath, then cooked in huge vats of live steam. The kernels, freed of their fibrous outside layers and nutritious germs, were then mixed with a refined sugar syrup which contained some of the vitamins that had been removed in the beginning, and flavorings to fill out the now bland flavor of the cereal, crushed with heavy rollers, dried and toasted in an oven, and then shaken into their brightly colored boxes, which had BHA and BHT (antioxidants) added to keep the paper-like flakes from spoiling.

What is so tragic, I feel, is that this overprocessed pretender to the role of food is actually considered nutritious by millions of people. By comparison with artificially colored puffs of sugar or chemical-laden, sugar filled pastries, perhaps; by comparison with real, honest-to-goodness food, no.

But don't proper breakfasts take an age to prepare? I know the question well — there were years when I was frequently seen downing a glass of instant breakfast and dribbling crumbs of toasted pastry on my car seat as I raced to work because I thought I didn't have time to fix anything more substantial. Or because I really didn't think it mattered a whole lot. Or because I was dieting, and didn't feel like eating breakfast anyway.

Thanks to friends who knew better, and to people like contributors to *Mother Earth News* and *Organic Gardening and Farming*, however, people who cared about food and the state of our health, I eventually learned that a four-minute egg and a piece of whole wheat toast can be washed down with a glass of reconstituted frozen orange juice (or even of fresh orange juice) in just about the same amount of time it took me to prepare my synthetic breakfasts of old.

And with only a little more planning in the morning I can serve hot whole grain cereal (made from grains without preservatives or sugar added), toast, and fresh fruit to everyone in the family. And still get us all out of the house on time.

A trip to a food co-op or large natural food store will provide you with a wonderful selection of whole grain cereals, both cold and hot. Cream of rye, similar to oatmeal but with a richer flavor, is one of my favorites. Others, good for the smallest child, are rice cream (ground whole brown rice), muesli (quick cooking oats combined with ground nuts and seeds and raisins), and nine grain cereal (finely ground multigrain cereal). There are boxes of cold cereal such as whole grain puffed brown rice, puffed whole corn, puffed whole wheat, and puffed whole millet, raisin bran without preservatives and with less sugar than the supermarket variety, and numerous brands of granola, a cooked oat and nut cereal (although watch out for the sugar content on those — it can be quite high).

58

Pancake and waffle mixes can be found in several combinations of whole grains; muffin mixes, cornbread mixes, and even bread mixes can be used to create nutritious breakfasts without arising at 5:00 a.m. to do so. Some careful label reading can net you an armload of boxes of breakfast fixings without preservatives, artificial colors, artificial flavors, and most without sugar.

You can also shop to avoid certain grains if you have food allergies to contend with. One or two major brands specialize in biscuit, pancake, and bread mixes which do not contain wheat.

There is a book that someone gave me a few years ago which probably deserves quite a bit of the credit for the way I feel about breakfasts (and my English father who nagged me all the way through high school undoubtedly deserves the rest — but I'd never admit it). It is called *The Natural Breakfast Book*, and it was written by the editors of Rodale Press. They tell you how to make nutritious cereals and baked goods, but also how to create innovative and tasty breakfasts which might put some of the motivation back into you and your family to eat more carefully in the morning.

After all, breakfast is where it all begins, right?

BREAKFAST MUFFINS

2 cups whole wheat flour
½ teaspoon salt
1½ teaspoons baking powder
1 teaspoon cinnamon
½ cup chopped dates
¼ cup chopped almonds
¼ cup sesame seeds
1 egg, beaten
¼ cup apple juice
1 cup cold milk
2 tablespoons oil

Stir together flour, salt, cinnamon and baking powder; add dates, nuts and seeds to the flour mixture. In another bowl, beat egg and stir in milk, juice and oil. Add dry ingredients just until blended. Fill greased muffin tins ⅔ full. Bake for 20 to 25 minutes at 350°F. Makes 12.

MUESLI

This uncooked oat cereal is the invention of Swiss nutritionist Bircher-Benner, who felt that a diet rich in fresh and dried fruit, nuts, and grains was the secret to consistent good health. It is meant to be eaten raw, with an ample amount of milk allowed to soak for five to ten minutes, and topped with a selection of fresh fruit (grated apples are my favorite).

    3 cups quick cooking oats
    1 cup chopped dried apple, pear, apricot
        or peach slices
    1 cup raisins or dates or both
    1 cup rye or wheat flakes, chopped
        in a blender
    ½ cup sunflower seed meal
    ½ cup sesame seeds
    ½ cup ground almonds and/or filberts
    ½ cup mild honey, warmed slightly

Combine all ingredients except the honey, then pour it in slowly, stirring constantly with a wooden spoon, blending it evenly.

Refrigerate muesli in a tightly covered container. Serve about ¼ cup with half a cup of milk. Add fresh fruit; let soak for ten minutes before eating. Enjoy.

FEATHER LIGHT WAFFLES

    1 cup whole grain flour
    2 teaspoons baking powder
    ½ teaspoon salt
    2 eggs
    1 cup cultured buttermilk or yoghurt
    1 tablespoon vegetable oil

Stir together dry ingredients, pressing out lumps. Beat eggs slightly; add with liquid and oil to flour. Thin with milk if necessary to reach a pourable consistency. Bake on hot greased waffle iron (use saturated fats or liquid lecithin for greasing griddles and pans; healthful low-cholesterol oils let things stick).

Note: These are good made with freshly ground barley flour, whole wheat flour, or a combination of wheat and rye, wheat and oats, or wheat and barley. Experiment.

PEANUT BUTTER MILK

A variety of "instant" breakfasts can be made with your blender and a little imagination. (Check the Beverage section for other ideas.) This one is a children's special, and works well when we're late for soccer practice or dancing lessons on Saturday morning, or only have ten minutes between getting up and getting to the school bus.

For each serving, combine at high speed:

1 cup milk
1 tablespoon smooth peanut butter
1 ripe banana
1 tablespoon protein powder

FRESHLY CRUNCHED GRANOLA

This is just a starter recipe — add or delete ingredients to meet your family's tastes. Make a batch and keep it cool and dry, and it will last for several weeks.

6 cups rolled old fashioned oats
1 cup shredded unsweetened coconut
1 cup fresh raw wheat germ
½ cup sunflower seeds
¼ cup sesame seeds
½ cup chopped nuts
½ cup unrefined vegetable oil
½ cup honey
¼ cup hot water
1½ teaspoon salt
1 teaspoon pure vanilla
1 cup raisins or chopped dates

Combine oats, coconut, wheat germ, sunflower seeds, sesame seeds and nuts in a large bowl. Stir together oil and honey with the hot water, then stir in salt and vanilla. Pour this mixture over the grains, stirring thoroughly. Spread mixture on cookie sheets in a thin layer, and toast at 325°F for 25 to 30 minutes, stirring often. The oats should be crisp and brown, the coconut not burned. Allow to cool thoroughly, then add raisins and place in an airtight container for storage. Serve cold with milk for breakfast.

EGG IN A WINDOW

A memory from Girl Scout Camp; my children love it.

Melt a pat of butter over low heat in a large flat-bottomed skillet. Cut a two-inch square out of the center of a slice of whole grain bread (one slice for each egg). Place the bread in the pan and break a small or medium egg into the hole.

Cook until the egg is ready to turn, then carefully flip, retaining the egg in the hole as you turn it. These are best soft-cooked, so the liquid egg yolk can be used to soak the bread as it is eaten. The squares can all be toasted at the end and used to wipe the plates clean.

LUNCH IS SIMPLE

What is lunch? At our house it is a coming together — Doña Ana from her studies, John from nursery school, and Mama from her typewriter. On weekends I feel like a wagon train cook with a triangle, summoning D.A. from her art project or her carpentry, her brother from the sandbox, and big John from his computer. Sometimes the cats, dog, and chickens come running too, sure that I have enough to feed a few extra mouths.

We eat and talk, and usually are in a hurry to get back to whatever it was we were doing, or on to whatever we thought about on the way home from school. It's a refueling, a meeting of eyes and smiles (or tears), then a parting again, usually fairly quickly.

Our breakfasts and dinners are usually more leisurely. Sleepy in the morning or weary from the day's labors at night, we dawdle over several different courses and ask for second helpings. But lunch is over in a flash — and we're all apart again, leaving me with an empty house and a sink full of dishes.

I tend therefore to make lunches simple one-plate affairs which combine several food groups at once — and arrange the food on plates before calling in the troops, afraid that I'll forget items otherwise, after we get to talking about the morning's events.

Typical menus:

Tuna salad sandwich on whole wheat toast, milk, celery sticks stuffed with peanut butter, two cherry tomatoes, and four orange segments.

A bowl of tomato soup with cheese cubes floating in it, whole grain crackers with cream cheese, apple juice, and a small bunch of grapes.

Quesadillos, carob milk, carrot-raisin salad, and apple wedges.

Everyone is hungry at lunch time. Food goes down cheerfully. It seems to be an easy meal for us to eat.

How about lunch boxes? We've done that, too. I developed a formula that seemed to work well (and plugging items into the formula saved me from thinking too hard in the sleepiness of morning). Just choose at least one item from each category.

Protein (hardboiled egg, slice of cheese, nuts, peanut butter, meat, cream cheese, yoghurt)

*Complementing protein** (whole wheat crackers, corn nuts, toasted soybeans, sesame butter)

Fresh fruit or vegetable (banana, apple, celery, peach, etc.)

Beverage (usually fruit juice — milk in thermos bottles doesn't seem to stay cold enough)

Something to Trade (whole wheat animal crackers made with honey, raisins, trail mix, half a carob candy bar)

Younger children don't seem to fare too well with traditional sandwich lunches, and even older children enjoy a change from them. Plastic bags or plastic containers keep fresh foods crisp and attractive. A note which says "I love you" or "Have a good Thursday" make the connection between you and the lunchbox a little closer.

Children can help to make their own lunches at an early age — three or four years old — and when they choose which kind of cracker, or whether to have carrots or celery, they are more likely to eat their lunch when mealtime comes. Sometimes all they need to do is put your selections into the plastic boxes, or help you screw the top onto the thermos, to feel part of the process.

The extra time spent letting a small child help will be paid back when he or she is six, seven, or eight — a child of that age can make his or her lunch alone. You still set the guidelines (try posting a formula such as the above), and provide the food choices, then give your children the responsibility of fitting the choices into the guidelines. Eventually your chores become a little lighter, and they have learned a bit of nutrition.

QUESADILLOS

A speedy lunch for a crowd. For each sandwich, use one corn tortilla, buttered to the edges, and thinly sliced jack cheese to cover.

Place tortillas under a broiler until the cheese is melted and bubbling. Remove from broiler and sprinkle with chopped onion, tomatoes, chiles, lettuce (all prepared ahead), and fold tortilla in half, working quickly so that the cheese sticks the sandwich together as it cools.

---

*Refer to the chart on page 91 for help in complementing proteins.

These are delicious even without the trimmings — just plain cheese.

MEXICAN PIZZAS

1 dozen corn or whole wheat tortillas
1 8-ounce can tomato sauce
1 pound jack cheese, grated
½ pound mushrooms, sliced
sunflower seeds

Sauté mushrooms lightly in a small amount of butter. Meanwhile, roast tortillas in the oven until dry on both sides but not crisp. Spread each tortilla with 1 tablespoon tomato sauce. Sprinkle mushrooms and sunflower seeds over it, and cover with a generous handful of grated cheese.

Place under broiler until cheese is bubbly and flecked with brown. Cool slightly before serving.

TUNAFISH CUPS

1 6-ounce can of tuna for each 4 servings
grated carrots
chopped bell pepper
onions chopped very fine
celery sliced very thin
raw green beans sliced crosswise finely
1 teaspoon powdered soup mix (see appendix)
1-2 tablespoons mayonnaise

Blend ingredients, or a reasonable approximation thereof (this one is easy to fake). Spoon mixture into bell pepper halves or whole ripe tomatoes hollowed out (if you use tomatoes, chop the pulp and add that to the mixture also.) Serve at once.

HUMMOUS SPREAD

Hummous, a staple in Lebanon and other Mediterranean countries, is a creamy spread made from garbanzo beans. Spread on crackers or whole grain bread, this makes a great lunch or after-school snack.

    2 cups cooked garbanzo beans (chick-peas)
    juice of one lemon
    2 tablespoons sesame or olive oil
    1 teaspoon salt
    1 teaspoon raw sesame seeds or sesame
        butter (tahini)

Mash garbanzos well with a wooden spoon or heavy fork, or buzz in a blender; stir in oil until the consistency is spreadable (you may need slightly more or less oil depending upon the moisture content of the chick-peas). Add salt and sesame seeds and blend thoroughly. This can be stored in a covered container in the refrigerator and used for several days.

EAT YOUR SALAD FIRST

One of the simplest tricks to keeping the waistlines small and the children eating their vegetables is to serve a salad at the beginning of the meal — and spike it with nutritious foods.

My family is usually so hungry when they first sit down that you could offer them french fried sand and I think they would eat it. If the choice instead is colorful greens tossed with several attractive vegetables and moistened with a well-chosen dressing, they will inhale enough nutrition before I even serve the main course to last them for several hours.

And for those of us who often eat too much, the chance to gorge on lots of fresh raw vegetables satisfies the craving without adding too many calories to the day's total.

Salads are frequently ignored in the rush of daily meals, yet once they are prepared and on the table, I think most of us would rather eat them than many other items, especially when the weather is hot. The step to bypass seems to be thinking it's too much trouble. So make it interesting for yourself.

Start by using different greens. Anything which is leafy and green (almost — don't use rhubarb leaves; they're poisonous) is fair game. Tear pieces of romaine, butter lettuce, iceburg, spinach, swiss chard, endive, chicory. I usually use at least three different greens. Mustard greens, beet leaves, celery tops, parsley, cilantro, cabbage. Taste the leaves. If they are bitter, make the pieces tiny, or use less of them. Avoid cutting the greens — the brown edges you will find the next day are the result of oxidation brought on by the use of metal blades, and signals vitamin loss. Tear the leaves, and you can use them the next day if you should have some left.

After putting a goodly number of greens into your bowl, start decorating them with colorful vegetables. Tomatoes, radishes, avocado, of course, if they are in season and available, but how about daikon, jicama, turnips, or parsnips? Daikon is a giant Japanese radish, sometimes hot, always tasty. Jicama hails from south of the border, and is sweet and moist — sliced into small squares a quarter of an inch thick it provides a real variety flavor for your salad. Turnips and parsnips usually are in the category of vegetables people don't think they like, but you might surprise yourself if you try them raw.

Other possibilities for salad vegetables are cauliflower pieces, broccoli slices, cucumber cubes, mushroom slices, asparagus florets, bell pepper strips and carrots, sliced or chopped. Unless you have very tiny children in your midst, or are struggling with false teeth, avoid grating vegetables into the salad bowl. That creates so much surface area, and vitamin loss occurs along the exposed surfaces. Vitamin C, bioflavonoids, and the B vitamins are lost in water, and in air vegetables lose Vitamins A, C and E. The more surface area, the greater the loss.

A word about preparation of greens and other vegetables. Try to get your salad fixings as fresh as possible, of course, and then refrigerate them right away. Vitamin loss is slowed in low temperatures. Wash the vegetables in cold water, but do not soak, or the vitamins will go down the drain. Dry thoroughly, using either turkish towels, paper towels, or centrifugal action. Swinging your greens in a net bag will dry them effectively. If you do not plan to serve them immediately, refrigerate everything again in plastic bags or airtight containers. This will provide the crispest, tastiest and most vitamin-rich selection for your table.

The late Adelle Davis (*Let's Cook It Right*) said to apply oil (preservative-free unrefined oil, of course) to your salad, thoroughly coating each leaf and vegetable, before adding herbs, spices, or acid (lemon juice or vinegar) to the bowl. The reason for this is that if moisture is added first, the oil will not adhere, and if the oil does not adhere evenly the herbs will clump. Another reason for coating everything with oil is to seal out the vitamin-destroying moisture and air.

But Adelle Davis (and Julia Child) notwithstanding, we cannot all manage to toss and dress each salad at the table. The confusion which reigns in my house at dinner time cannot possibly be a unique event, and attempting to balance oil, vinegar, lemon juice and six herbs while

68

feeding a toddler, cutting up another child's meat, answering the telephone and not tripping over the dog is a feat I simply have not often managed.

So we compromise. Nutritionally, salad greens do benefit from being coated lightly with oil before being submitted to the caustic effects of acids such as lemon juice or vinegar. Water and air do deplete greens of their vitamins, and acid contributes still more trauma for the poor salad, so the oil is really very important. I lean towards olive oil, sesame oil, or sunflower oil for my salads, but experiment with several different ones or blends of two or three until you find your favorite.

If you are going to make your own dressing at the table, add about half as much vinegar or lemon juice as you used oil (toss the greens well after the oil, to coat everything evenly, then toss them again lightly after the vinegar). Sprinkle the salad now with your herbs — I use parsley, thyme, marjoram, and sweet basil, but also good is a tiny amount of fresh mint. Dill, oregano, and sage are other possibilities. Toss again.

However, if as we often do, you are using a pre-mixed dressing, coat the greens with a little oil, then dress. We make our own dressings whenever we can, using a base of yoghurt and mayonnaise for the cream dressings and sunflower oil and vinegar or lemon juice for the others, but there are a number of commercial salad dressings now available which do not contain chemical additives or preservatives, and if you read labels carefully you will find some which match your family's tastes.

The dressing does not have to stop with the herbs or the bottle, however. To make each salad special, and add even more nutritional value to it, sprinkle cubes of cheese and chopped nuts and seeds over the salad just before serving. Good choices are sesame, sunflower or pumpkin seeds, almonds, cashews, chopped walnuts or pecans, and filberts. Raw, often unsprayed, shelled nuts can be purchased in natural food stores (search for a store which carries them in bulk — they are much cheaper that way).

Cheeses can vary as much as your taste — we like cubes of Swiss, cheddar, jack, and gouda — this might be a place to help your family learn to like cheese if they do not do so now. If you are uncertain about the tastes of your guests, place some of the larger nuts and seeds and the cubes of cheese in separate small bowls surrounding the salad bowl. Place a spoon in each one and lead the rest by serving yourself from each one to show how it's done.

In Europe the salad is often served after the main course, not as an accompaniment to the rest of the meal, but as a special dish in its own right. You might wish to try that — we often find that a well-prepared salad will serve as a dessert in our home. On the other hand, try sometimes to serve a nutritionally complete salad first, and you may discover that you have just served an entire meal in one course!

CREAMY AVOCADO DRESSING

1 medium ripe avocado
½ – 1 cup plain yoghurt
juice of one lemon
½ teaspoon salt (to taste)
½ teaspoon crumbled dill weed
½ teaspoon crushed thyme

Peel and mash the avocado. Add about the same amount of yoghurt as you have avocado puree — more if you prefer a tangy dressing. Stir in lemon juice, salt and herbs. Coat salad lightly with vegetable oil, tossing to coat evenly, then stir in this dressing or serve separately in a bowl.

TABULI SALAD

This version of a traditional Middle Eastern dish makes a refreshing lunch. I enjoy the flavor of fresh mint, and cultivate a patch by a leaky faucet so that I always have it available. If that herb isn't one of your favorites, omit it and you'll find the taste of the salad is entirely different.

½ cup cracked wheat or bulgur
3 ripe tomatoes, finely chopped
½ cucumber, finely chopped
4 green onions, finely chopped
¼ cup chopped fresh parsley
2 tablespoons chopped fresh mint
4 tablespoons olive oil
2 tablespoons lemon juice
1 – 2 teaspoons salt
¼ teaspoon freshly ground ginger

Cover grain with boiling water and let soak while preparing vegetables. Drain thoroughly, stir into bowl, and chill for several hours. When ready to serve, drain again and serve on a bed of finely torn crisp greens.

SPINACH AND MUSHROOM SALAD

    2 tangerines, segmented (or one can
        mandarin oranges, drained)
    ¼ red onion, thinly sliced
    1 cup fresh mushrooms, sliced
    4 cups fresh spinach, washed and torn

Dressing:

    ½ cup vegetable oil
    ¼ cup lemon juice
    ½ teaspoon salt
    pinch of pepper
    1 teaspoon honey

Combine above ingredients (reserving 2 tablespoons of the oil) and chill.

Combine tangerine or orange segments with onions, mushrooms and spinach in salad bowl. Cover and chill until ready to serve. Coat salad with two tablespoons of oil, then pour dressing over the salad, reserving remainder for another time. Serve.

MARINATED BEAN SALAD

One cup each of three or four of the following cooked, drained beans:

    soybeans
    garbanzos (chick-peas)
    lima beans
    kidney beans
    cut green beans
    navy beans
    wax beans
    Any other small legume

For each cup of beans, add the following:

    3 tablespoons vegetable oil
    1 tablespoon vinegar
    ¼ teaspoon salt
    ¼ teaspoon pepper
    ¼ teaspoon marjoram
    ¼ teaspoon basil
    ¼ teaspoon dry mustard
    ¼ teaspoon honey

71

(The last seven ingredients may be blended together and added to bean mixture after the oil is stirred in.)

Stir ingredients together thoroughly, cover tightly, and refrigerate for at least 24 hours. Drain and serve on a bed of greens.

CITRUS AND SPROUT SALAD

This salad can be adjusted according to the availability and cost of citrus fruits. I prefer a combination of grapefruit, Valencia oranges, and tangerines.

    Several citrus fruits — grapefruit, oranges,
        tangelos, tangerines, mandarin oranges
    Plain yoghurt
    Fresh alfalfa or clover sprouts
    Raisins (optional)
    Nuts (optional)

Peel and segment the fruit, then cut each segment into two or three crosswise pieces (except mandarin oranges). Place in a bowl and stir in (gently) enough yoghurt to fairly well coat the chunks. If you are including raisins and nuts, stir them in at this time — chop the nuts coarsely. Refrigerate for about one hour to blend flavors.

Serve by placing a bed of sprouts on a plate and spooning the mixture over it.

GARBANZO PEA SALAD

    1 15-ounce can garbanzo beans
    1 cup fresh or frozen green peas
    ¼ cup raw sunflower seeds
    1 tablespoon fresh mint (optional)
    2 tablespoons mayonnaise or yoghurt

Stir together. This can be served immediately on a bed of lettuce or alfalfa sprouts if the peas are frozen. Otherwise, chill before serving.

FRESH FRUIT AMBROSIA SALAD

 4 cups fresh fruit chunks (apples,
   peaches, apricots, strawberries,
   pears, melons, oranges, pineapple —
   remove pits or cores, but do not peel.
 ¼ cup raw almonds
 ¼ cup raw cashews
 ¼ cup coconut, shredded or large flakes
 ¼ cup sunflower, pumpkin, sesame or
   flax seeds (or a combination)
 ½ cup plain or vanilla yoghurt

Stir ingredients gently together, being careful not to crush fruit. Chill thoroughly before serving. This can be served on crisp greens or directly into small bowls.

SOUPS, HOT AND COLD

Soups and stews are a staple at our house. Every Sunday I make soup and fresh bread, and the leftovers often serve during the week for lunches and quick dinners, or to supplement otherwise sketchy meals.

Creating your own soup stock and freezing it whenever you have a sufficiency of bones or vegetable trimmings makes soupmaking quite easy. While the stock is heating, rummage around in your refrigerator for leftover cooked cereal, beans, vegetables, pieces of meat too small to make sandwiches. Add some whole grain alphabets, or noodles — some uncooked grain or beans if you have time (30 to 60 minutes). Taste. Season with herbs. Add a can or jar of stewed tomatoes to make gumbo. Chop some fresh vegetables or take some from the freezer. Add them just in time so they are still pretty and slightly crisp at serving time. Soup can be a whole meal, and often is, in our home.

For a long time, however, I felt that soup was great in the winter, but suspended soup-making activites when it got hot. Then one day I tasted Vichyssoise (basically a cold potato and cream soup). I didn't know it at the time, but that soup was about to change our summer eating habits. Gazpacho came next. That soup wasn't cream based, but used tomato juice instead. Raw vegetables and chiles chopped into the icy juice made a refreshing lunch, and I was hooked.

I began searching for new recipes. Finding very few, I discovered that soups which are traditionally served hot can often be chilled with excellent (and elegant) results. For an example, try cream of asparagus soup. I discovered how good that tasted cold by accident one day when, finding leftover soup in the refrigerator, I decided it was too hot a day to light the stove. Vegetable soups especially seem improved by chilling — add a little cream to leftover broccoli, cucumber or mushroom soup and discover a new treat.

Other soups which lend themselves to being served cold are legume and nut soups. Combined with milk, yoghurt, or cream, legumes and nuts form complete proteins, and so these are excellent choices when the soup will be the main portion of the meal, as at lunch. Nut soups include creamy almond, hazelnut (filbert), or Brazil nut; legume soups which I have tried chilled have been cream of peanut, split pea with yoghurt, and black bean.

Cook your soups at night when it is cooler, or choose a cool day or weekend to prepare the soup, then freeze until you need it. An exception to that is gazpacho, which is not cooked at all, but merely mixed together raw, and can be made quickly on the hottest days.

The texture of most cold soups should be creamy, almost silky. You can manage that sometimes by mixing them in a blender, but if your soup contains something gritty like cucumber seeds or nuts, it helps to press the mixture through a sieve. That doesn't take as long as it sounds, actually. I used to avoid that kind of "from scratch" cooking until I discovered how simple it really was and how much difference it made to the results.

CREAMY ALMOND SOUP

2 cups shelled almonds
1 cup milk
¼ cup whole wheat bread crumbs
2 tablespoons butter
2 tablespoons whole wheat pastry flour
4 cups chicken or vegetable stock
¼ teaspoon ground mace
1 teaspoon salt (unless stock is salty)
¼ teaspoon pepper
1 cup cream

Put almonds through a nut grinder or grate in a Mouli grater (a blender works fairly well also); stir into milk and simmer gently until nuts are soft. Stir in the bread crumbs and mix well. Press through a sieve. Melt butter; blend in flour. Add stock gradually, stirring to prevent lumps. Stir in the almond mixture; add seasoning. Simmer for five minutes, stirring constantly. Chill thoroughly. Blend in cream just before serving.

LAMB AND GRAIN STEW

Many soups can be cooked in a crock pot, and this is one of them; adjust the amounts to fit your appliance. I like to cook the meat one day and refrigerate it overnight so we can remove the hardened fat from the surface. The stock and bones can then be returned to a regular soup pot and the vegetables and grains cooked the next night.

    2 pounds lamb shoulder or neck
    4 quarts cold water
    ¼ cup coarsely cracked corn
    ¼ cup coarsely cracked wheat
    ⅛ cup coarsely cracked rye
    1 small turnip, chopped
    4 medium carrots, chopped
    2 stalks celery, chopped
    1 medium onion, chopped
    3 teaspoons salt

Wipe meat with a damp paper towel and place in a large soup pot. Cover with water, bring to a boil, and simmer, covered, for one or two hours, or until tender. Skim fat from broth, or refrigerate overnight, and lift fat from top before reheating. Add grains and chopped vegetables, season with salt, simmer for another hour, and serve with chunks of whole grain bread.

CREAM OF PEANUT SOUP

We first tasted this soup in restored Williamsburg, Virginia, where it was served to us in lovely tureens by eighteenth-century serving maids. Peanuts, which are legumes, have the nutritional value and taste of beans when served this way.

    2 stalks celery, chopped
    1 small onion, chopped
    ¼ cup butter
    1 tablespoon peanut or whole wheat flour
    4 cups chicken stock
    1 cup peanut butter
    1 pint thick cream

Sauté celery and onion in butter until quite tender. Add flour and cook, stirring constantly, until evenly blended. Add stock and bring to a boil. Stir in peanut butter. Cook slowly until celery and onion can be smashed easily against the side of the pan. Stir in cream and serve.

CREAM OF BROCCOLI SOUP

Cook two heads of broccoli in ½ cup water until fork-tender. Drain, saving broth. Melt 6 tablespoons butter. Stir in 6 tablespoons whole wheat pastry flour or unbleached flour. Add reserved broth, 1 pint milk and 1 pint cream.

Using half of the broccoli, whirl cooked mixture in a blender after adding 1 teaspoon herb salt and two tablespoons vegetable boullion powder (Vigor Cup). Chop the remainder of the broccoli and add to soup. Heat to serving temperature.

This is good served with wedges of lemon in each bowl. It's also good chilled.

76

QUICK CLAM CHOWDER

1 small can minced clams in water or clam
  juice
1 medium can whole baby clams in water or
  clam juice
3 small potatoes, scrubbed but not peeled
About 1 quart milk (or part cream, if you
  want to be fancy)
1 to 2 tablespoons unbleached flour
parsley
thyme
cinnamon

Drain both cans of clams, reserving liquid. Cook potatoes, cubed into ½ inch pieces, in 3 cups of milk and liquid from clams. When tender, add clams and season with fresh or dried parsley, thyme, and a pinch of cinnamon.

Blend 1 tablespoon flour with a little milk. Stir into soup and continue stirring constantly until it returns to the boil and thickens. If you want your soup thicker, repeat with another tablespoon of flour and more milk. If you want it thinner, stir in more milk.

HOT DOG BEAN SOUP

A favorite of our children.

1 cup navy beans, soaked overnight in 8 cups water
1 large onion, finely chopped
2-3 carrots, diced
2 stalks celery, diced
1 tablespoon butter
1 tablespoon whole grain flour
½ cup water or milk
2-3 nitrate-free frankfurters, sliced*

Boil beans, onions, carrots, and celery in water over low heat until all are tender, at least 2 hours. Remove ½ cup beans from pan and squash them into a creamy texture with a wooden spoon. Melt butter; stir in flour, then add squashed beans and about ½ cup water or milk, stirring until smooth. Cook for 2 minutes, stirring constantly, then add to soup and simmer 15 minutes. Stir in sliced franks, heat through, and serve. Salt to taste.

---

*Nitrate-free hot dogs can be obtained from the freezer of some supermarkets and most natural food stores.

CREAM OF MUSHROOM SOUP

1 pound mushrooms, cleaned and finely chopped
1 onion, finely chopped
1 or 2 stalks of celery, finely chopped
4 tablespoons butter
4 cups chicken stock or water
4 tablespoons unbleached or whole wheat pastry
    flour
2 cups milk
salt and herbs to taste

Sauté the mushrooms, onion, and celery in butter until translucent and quite soft. Add stock or water, bringing to a boil and simmering for 20 minutes or so. Combine flour and milk in blender container with one or two cups of the soup; blend until vegetables are liquified and return to the pot. Stir until soup returns to boiling and thickens. If you would like the soup thicker, return two cups of hot soup to blender, add 1 or 2 tablespoons more flour, blend, and repeat above step.

If you want to use mushroom soup in a recipe calling for a can of unreconstituted cream of mushroom soup, make the above recipe with 2 cups of stock, 1 cup of milk, and the same amount of everything else.

CREAM OF CHICKEN SOUP

Use above recipe, but omit mushrooms; blend entire soup until liquified before adding milk and flour; add 1 cup of chopped chicken and heat thoroughly before serving.

BORSCHT

10 small cooked beets (skin after cooking)
2 cups water
1 tablespoon honey
3 tablespoons vinegar
1 tablespoon finely chopped onion

Combine ingredients in a blender and chill thoroughly. Season to taste with salt, pepper, dill, or fennel, and serve topped with slices of hard cooked eggs.

78

LEEK AND WATERCRESS SOUP

1 large potato
4 sliced leeks
1 bunch fresh watercress

Cube potato; cook watercress, potato and leeks in a quart of water until tender. Put through blender (just to chop, not to puree). Season to taste. Chill.

VICHYSSOISE

1 large potato
4 cups chicken stock
2 tablespoons butter
1 medium onion
nutmeg
salt
chives
heavy cream

Cube potato and simmer in broth until tender. Sauté onion in butter until tender and golden; puree potato and onion in blender, season with nutmeg and salt, chill for several hours. Just before serving, stir in about a cup of cream and sprinkle with chives. Enjoy.

HUNGARIAN CUCUMBER SOUP

2-3 medium onions, finely chopped
¼ pound butter
2 Armenian cucumbers or 4 domestic, scrubbed
    and cubed (peel if waxed)
4-6 cups chicken stock
½ cup fresh parsley
2 large potatoes, scrubbed and chopped
1 cup plain yoghurt or thick cream

Sauté chopped onions in butter until soft and golden. Simmer cucumbers, potatoes and parsley until quite tender. Drain and combine with first mixture (save stock). Blend onions, cucumbers, one cup of reserved stock, potatoes and parsley in a blender (or put vegetables through a food mill, omitting liquid). If not velvet in texture, put puree through a sieve to remove pieces of skin and seeds. Return to blender and add stock until soup is of a creamy thickness. Chill thoroughly. Just before serving, stir in yoghurt or cream and top with chopped chives or finely chopped raw cucumber.

GAZPACHO

 4 large ripe tomatoes, blanched and peeled
 1 large cucumber (peeled if waxed)
 1 small onion
 1 bell pepper, seeded
 ½ cup wine vinegar or lemon juice
 ½ cup olive oil
 1 teaspoon chile sauce or tabasco
 1 teaspoon salt
 ½ teaspoon black pepper, freshly ground
    if possible
 3-4 cloves garlic
 2-3 cups tomato juice or V-8

Chop all vegetables into small cubes. Add remaining ingredients and press through a food mill or blend in an electric blender. Serve chilled with cucumber and tomato chunks floating in the bowls. An alternative is to simply chop the vegetables finely and not to puree them at all.

VEGETABLES

For some reason, vegetables have come to be the poor relations in most American meals. My personal theory is that it is because so few of them are eaten fresh any more, and because frozen, canned, and dehydrated vegetables frequently fall short of the flavor and texture of the fresh items.

Some vegetables hold up to freezing; many don't. I usually keep corn, peas, beans, and broccoli in the freezer for emergencies, but carrots, cauliflower, asparagus, lettuce, and many more must be purchased from a good produce market.

We serve two or three vegetables at every lunch and dinner, but at least one of them is raw. The number goes up drastically in the summer when our garden brings us radishes, lettuce, tomatoes, cucumber, etc. Cucumber slices, celery spread with cream cheese or nut butter, raw green beans, carrots, turnips, jicama — all these can be served as part of the meal, either on individual plates or in one main dish in the center of the table.

Serving vegetables raw can bring some pleasant surprises. Turnips, for example. Very few families admit to liking cooked turnips. Yet crisp slices of turnips always disappear quickly from my vegetable plate — even to visitors. And children or husbands who won't eat unusual vegetables, or cabbage family products, will often eat them when they are served attractively with other, more familiar vegetables, and with a yoghurt or salad dressing dip.

We enjoy dressing up vegetables, making them into souffles, dumplings, stir-fry combinations with nuts and seeds, or other such things. All you need to do to fill out the meal, then, is cook some soup, a stew, or a casserole, and you have a complete meal. There's not too many specific recipes, but here are a few ideas to get you started:

STIR-FRIED ASPARAGUS OR BROCCOLI

Wash and snap ends from asparagus stalks. (Slice broccoli lengthwise into quarters.) Heat oriental-style sesame oil in heavy skillet or wok; stir-fry vegetables until warmed all the way through, but still crisp. Sprinkle with brown sesame seeds and serve.

RAW VEGETABLE SAMPLER

Scrub and slice a variety of in-season vegetables, including some which are unusual and/or hard to get your family to eat when cooked. Peel only if skin is bitter, or woody, or otherwise unpalatable.

Put dressings, homemade or commercial without artificial ingredients, into bell peppers or tomatoes which have been hollowed out.

Surround with cut vegetables. Sprinkle a variety of nuts, seeds, and cubed cheeses over vegetables.

BAKED WINTER SQUASH

Halve squash. Remove seeds (save for roasting and snacking).

Place cut side down in pan of water and bake at 375° for 30 minutes. Meanwhile, melt butter, maple syrup or honey, and cinnamon together (I'm intentionally not giving amounts — use a little of each, to taste). Spoon mixture into cooked squash halves and return to the oven for fifteen more minutes, or until tender.

PESTO a la GENOVESE (Fresh Basil Sauce)

3 cups fresh basil leaves
3 cloves garlic, finely chopped
½ cup Italian parsley (cilantro)
½ cup olive oil
3 tablespoons butter
1 cup grated Parmesan or Romano cheese

Chop basil, parsley and garlic very fine. Meanwhile, heat oil and butter and cook chopped vegetables in this mixture for five to ten minutes. Add 4 tablespoons of hot water. Serve this green sauce over vegetables or pasta,* sprinkled generously with the cheese.

Toss gently. Enjoy. And remember to plant basil next year. (This sauce can be frozen for winter use.)

CABBAGE al dente (a la Joe Carcione)

Wash a head of Chinese cabbage — cut into quarters. Steam for five to ten minutes, until color brightens, but leaves are not yet limp. Sprinkle with raw cashews and serve.

BARLEY AND CARROTS

Cook hulled barley in vegetable stock until soft but still slightly chewy, about 30 minutes. Scrub but do not peel several carrots, and slice fairly thin. Stir-fry in vegetable oil until just tender. Drain barley (save stock for soup!). Stir in carrots and serve.

This is very good cold, with a little yoghurt stirred in.

---

*Many forms of pasta are available made from whole grain flour. Check your co-op or natural food store for noodles, lasagne, spaghetti, alphabets and others.

STUFFED ZUCCHINI

This is for the end of the season, when the zucchini are getting out of control and are about two feet long. By then they're so tough you need to take the seeds out to eat them, so we devised this mixture to fill the hole.

Halve lengthwise two large zucchini. Scoop out seeds and pulp. Parboil shells three to five minutes in a large pot. Drain and sprinkle with salt and pepper.

1 medium onion, chopped
1 clove garlic, finely chopped
2 tablespoons butter
1 cup cooked lentils
1 cup cooked brown rice
¼ cup chopped nuts
1 teaspoon salt
½ teaspoon pepper

Sauté onion and garlic in butter until tender. Combine with lentils, rice, nuts and seasoning. Heap into zucchini. Bake 25 minutes at 350°F, or until squash is fork-tender. Really huge ones may take longer.

Variation: Mix 1 pound ground beef into above mixture. This makes a tasty meat loaf, also.

CREAMY CHEESE SAUCE

Serve over steamed vegetables.

1 tablespoon butter
1 cup milk
1 teaspoon cornstarch or 1½ teaspoons
    arrowroot powder
1 cup grated cheese
¼ teaspoon salt
¼ teaspoon dry mustard

Melt butter over low heat; stir in half of milk. Stir together remainder of milk with cornstarch or arrowroot until dissolved; stir into mixture in pan. Add cheese and stir frequently until cheese is melted and sauce comes just to the boil. Season with salt and mustard, adjusting to taste. Remove from heat and serve at once.

FAST DINNER — SPANISH RICE AND PEAS

cooked brown rice (as much of it as there are people)
tomato soup or tomato sauce
fresh or frozen peas

Moisten rice with soup or sauce in a skillet. Just use enough to color and flavor slightly — don't make it soupy. Stir in peas and heat just until warmed through. This is very attractive and tasty, and because the rice and peas are complementary proteins, also quite nutritious. Top with grated cheese for a nice touch.

LET THEM EAT STEAK

According to Ananda Marga, an international social service and meditation society, the word "vegetarian" does not come from "vegetable", but from the Latin word *vegetare*, meaning "to enliven". The person tagged a "vegetable eater" today was referred to by the Romans as *homo vegetus*, describing him as in vigorous and dynamic health.

Our society has traditionally depicted vegetarians as sickly, weak, and strange, and does not yet give much credence to the viability of living without meat. But Albert Einstein was a vegetarian. So were Tolstoy, Thoreau, Emerson, Benjamin Franklin, Louisa May Alcott, Sir Isaac Newton, Leonardo da Vinci, John Wesley, Albert Schweitzer, and many other people with strong minds.

Somehow, even though evidence is to the contrary, we typically think of vegetarians as being emotional rather than intellectual, mystical rather than reasoning, and perhaps because of this persisting belief in their esoteric nature we have not asked them how they feel after avoiding meat for 20, 30, even 60 or 70 years. We have not generally asked them how many colds they get each year, or how many of them die of heart disease or cancer, or how often they get heartburn, ulcers, diverticulitis, or are constipated.

I am not suggesting that we might discover vegetarianism to be the solution to all of these things, or even to any of them, just that we might inquire.

Some of the arguments for being a vegetarian leave me wishing for a physiology text or a chance to talk to some butchers, but there are some points made by Ananda Marga and others which appeal to me.

For example, the inefficiency of feeding grain to animals so that we can eat the animals, instead of eating the grain directly. (Grains in correct combination with beans, nuts, seeds, milk, etc., are nutritionally equivalent to meat protein.)

Such as the enduring good health and long lives of numerous vegetarian societies around the world. Such as the lower rates of heart disease, digestive and intestinal disorders, and cancer in vegetarian segments of our own society. Such as the incredibly high rate of contaminants in our meat, not only because of the natural results of decay, but also because of the high content of DDT and other chemicals that have accumulated in the animals during their lifetimes combined with the growth hormones, antibiotics, nitrates and nitrites which are injected into the flesh before we eat it.

But can a person eat well on only vegetables? That is the underlying consideration for most people objecting to removing meat from their diet. We have been conditioned to believe that we must eat steak to stay healthy, when the truth may actually be the reverse. There is a tremendous range of protein content in vegetarian food, running from eight percent in some cereal grains to 40 percent in soybeans. Even the leanest cut of steak has only 20 percent useable protein. Many nuts, seeds, and legumes contain 30 percent.

Also, a point which is often overlooked is that vegetarians do not rely on one or even two vegetables for their protein at each meal, but in a combination of several which, when eaten together, provide more than an adequate amount of high-quality protein.

In order to become a healthy and creative vegetarian cook, one needs to learn about protein and the complementing of amino acids. Vegetarian meals in other cultures naturally take these different protein contents into consideration, and combinations such as rice and beans, or beans and cheese, or tofu (soybean curd) and rice, or in Europe rye bread and cheese, have endured to this day.

A good text for learning about protein complementarity is Frances Moore Lappe's *Diet for a Small Planet*, and I would highly recommend it. A copy was given to me several years ago by a healthy vegetarian mother of healthy vegetarian children and it has radically changed my eating habits. Note the word "habits" — for such they were. I feel strongly that eating habits should be replaced by carefully thought out eating "patterns", and perhaps an inquiry into vegetarian eating patterns will help to influence your own.

A visit to your local library should introduce you to several new and valuable vegetarian cookbooks. One of my favorites is *Laurel's Kitchen*, by Laurel Robertson, Carol Flinders, and Bronwen Godfrey. It contains a complete section on vegetarian nutrition and explores ideas for gradually altering long-standing eating habits. Even if you continue to eat meat, learning which proteins best complement each other will help you to plan cost-effective and nutritious recipes to enhance your meat dishes.

One of the strongest arguments given for vegetarian eating is the lower rate of intestinal and digestive illnesses among vegetarians, as well as the lower rate of heart disease, cancer, and many other illnesses. I believe that this is a result, not simply of eating no meat, but of eating more grains, nuts, seeds and fruit in their unrefined form.

It has been shown that when people move from a heavy grain-eating culture into a western, refined-food culture, their incidence of these illnesses rapidly approaches the norm for that area. Eating meat does not necessarily cause these problems. Eating insufficient unrefined grains and fruits and vegetables does. So if you like meat, eat meat. But don't eat it for breakfast, lunch, and dinner.

If you want to eat meat, eat it sparingly, lovingly, and be careful where it comes from. Seek out independent farmers and people you know personally whenever possible, and assure yourself that the animals are healthy and well-fed as well as free from hormones, stimulants, and preservatives in any form.

Increase your consumption of unrefined breads and whole grain dishes, of fruits and vegetables in their natural states, and avoid the use of white flour, white rice, and white sugar. With some thoughtful planning, you can give yourself the advantages of a healthy vegetarian diet — and still not give up your meat.

MEALS WITHOUT MEAT

A family beginning to eat vegetarian meals is often at a loss for recipes. Here are several main dishes to get you started (Thanks to members of my cooking classes for several of them):

CHILE RELLENO WHOLE WHEAT CREPES

Crepes

   1 cup whole wheat pastry flour
   1½ cups milk
   3 eggs
   2 tablespoon melted butter, cooled
   ¼ teaspoon salt

Mix all ingredients together until smooth. Allow to rest in refrigerator for at least 1 hour or overnight. The batter should be like heavy cream.

Filling

7 ounce can milk whole chiles, cut in half
1 pound Monterey jack cheese

Prepare crepes. Set aside. Cut chiles into halves and wash to remove all seeds. Cut cheese into small pieces. Wrap each piece of cheese in a chile half and place on a crepe. Fold crepe into pockets and place seam-side down in a single layer in greased shallow pan.

The dish can be refrigerated at this point. When ready to bake, cover with sauce and extra cheese and bake at 350°F for 15-20 minutes until hot, and until the cheese melts.

Sauce

2 tomatoes, chopped
1 stalk celery, chopped
½ onion, chopped
½ chile, chopped
1 8-ounce can tomato sauce

Cook together and pour over rellenos. Makes about 12.

EASY EGGPLANT CASSEROLE

This depends for its color and speed upon a variety of cut vegetables, such as lima and Italian beans, cauliflower, baby carrots, broccoli and zucchini. I keep a bag of a vegetable combination called Mediterranean Vegetables in my freezer for last minute additions to soups, stews, omelettes or casseroles such as this. You can save money by preparing these vegetables for freezing yourself when you have time, but I find this way works well for me.

Peel and slice thinly one medium eggplant. Sauté in hot oil with a sliced onion. When soft, add one can stewed tomatoes (a pint, if home-canned), and enough frozen or freshly cut vegetables to add color and fill a shallow casserole of the right size to feed your family (I use a Corningware 9-inch for four people). Cover with grated jack cheese — lots. Heat in oven — 350°F — for 20 minutes or until cheese is melted. This reheats well.

TOFU PATTIES*

½ onion, minced
1 stalk celery, finely chopped
½ green pepper, finely chopped
2 tablespoons oil
1 package tofu** (about 20 ounces)
1 egg, beaten
2 tablespoons whole wheat flour
½ teaspoon salt
2 tablespoons soy sauce
2 teaspoons curry powder, OR ½ cup
   grated cheddar cheese
wheat germ, cornmeal, or sesame seeds

Chop the onion, celery, and green pepper finely and sauté it in oil until soft. Drain the tofu in a strainer; mash it with a fork and mix in the egg, flour, salt, and soy sauce. Add vegetables and either the curry powder or the cheese. Form into small patties and roll them in the wheat germ. Brown on a griddle or skillet, or bake in a 350°F oven. Makes about two dozen.

NOTE: Tofu, or soybean curd, can be purchased from the delicatessan section of most large supermarkets. Ask for delivery days and purchase it fresh.

CHILE CASSEROLE

2 4-ounce cans diced green chiles
1 pound Monterey jack cheese, coarsely grated
1 pound cheddar cheese, coarsely grated
4 egg whites
4 egg yolks
⅔ cup evaporated milk; undiluted
1 tablespoon flour
½ teaspoon salt
⅛ teaspoon pepper
2 sliced tomatoes

In a large bowl, combine grated cheeses and chiles. Turn into well-buttered shallow two-quart casserole. Beat egg whites until stiff. In a small bowl, combine egg yolks, milk, flour, salt and pepper until well-blended. Using a rubber spatula, fold beaten egg whites into egg yolk mixture. Pour egg mixture over cheese in casserole, and poke with fork to let it ooze through cheese. Bake 30 minutes at 325°F. Add tomatoes sliced on top and bake 30 minutes more.

---

*From *Laurel's Kitchen*, by Laurel Robertson, et al. Published by Nilgiri Press.

GREEN CHILE CHEESE CORNBREAD

3 eggs
2 cups buttermilk or yoghurt
⅓ cup unrefined vegetable oil
2 cups whole cornmeal
1 teaspoon salt
2 teaspoons baking powder
4 roasted, peeled, chopped long green chiles
1-2 cups grated sharp cheddar cheese

Mix together eggs, buttermilk, and oil. Stir together dry ingredients, pressing out lumps; add to liquid. Stir in chiles and all but ¼ cup of the cheese.

Preheat oven to 450°F. Heat oiled 10-inch cast iron skillet in oven. Pour in batter; top with remaining cheese. Bake 25-30 minutes, or until set and slightly brown on top. Cool slightly before cutting into wedges and serving with lots of butter.

POTATO CORN CAKES*

These cakes are delicious with applesauce and yoghurt. You may think that grating the potatoes and onion is a bother, but I'm convinced that grated vegetables make much lighter pancakes.

4 medium potatoes, scrubbed, with skins
1 large onion
2 eggs, beaten
1 tablespoon brewer's yeast
1 teaspoon salt
2 tablespoon whole wheat flour
1 tablespoon soy grits
1 cup milk powder (1⅓ cups if instant)
2 cups corn, fresh, frozen, or drained canned

Grate the potatoes and the onions (and please leave the potato skins on); stir in the eggs, brewer's yeast, salt, flour, and soy grits.

Carefully add the milk powder so that it doesn't lump too much (a few lumps don't matter).

Stir in the corn, and your cakes are ready to fry. Fry on an oiled griddle, browning them well on each side.

---

*From *Recipes for a Small Planet*, by Ellen Buchman Ewald. Published by Ballantine Books.

VEGETARIAN CASSEROLE ITALIANNE

Cooked brown rice
Cooked soybeans
1 pound ricotta cheese
Canned tomatoes in puree (large can).
    Canned tomatoes of any kind will do,
    but add a small can of puree in that case)
1 cup spinach
grated Romano cheese
salt, pepper, garlic, basil, rosemary, oregano

In 9" square greased casserole, place a layer of soybeans, spread with tomatoes, season with part of the herbs, then cover with ricotta cheese, spinach, and the remainder of the tomato. Add remaining herbs, cover with brown rice, and top with Romano cheese. Bake in moderate oven (350°F) 20 – 30 minutes.

BROWN RICE DELIGHT

To two cups boiling water add one cup brown rice. Simmer 35 minutes. Turn off heat. Let stand ten minutes without removing lid.

Into serving dish place ⅓ cup chopped celery and ⅓ cup chopped nuts, 1 tablespoon minced parsley, and 1 tablespoon minced red pepper or pimiento. Vary these amounts as you like.

Lift rice lid, quickly season (one tablespoon butter, ¼ teaspoon salt or vege-salt), and fork-fluff as you add ¼ to ½ cup frozen, uncooked petite peas. Add mixture to contents of serving dish. Season to taste, top with grated cheese. Melt cheese in a warm oven. Serve immediately.

WALNUT LOAF

1¾ cups milk
¼ cup vegetable oil
1½ cups whole wheat cracker crumbs
1 medium onion sliced thin and chopped
1 garlic clove, mashed
1 teaspoon dried oregano
2 cups ground nuts (almonds, walnuts, or pecans)
½ cup wheat germ
1 teaspoon salt
1 tablespoon soy sauce
½ cup tomato catsup
2 eggs, beaten

Sauté in oil the onion, garlic and oregano. Combine all remaining ingredients (ground nuts are better than chopped, which tend to become too dry). Shape into a loaf and bake at 350°F for 30 minutes. This loaf is not so firm as a meat loaf, so cut gently.

NOTE: to grind nuts, use a Mouli grater, an electric nut and seed mill, or a blender.

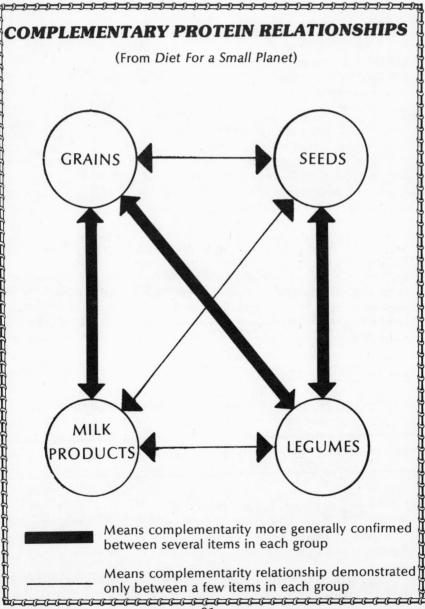

COMPLEMENTARY PROTEIN RELATIONSHIPS

(From *Diet For a Small Planet*)

GRAINS   SEEDS

MILK PRODUCTS   LEGUMES

Means complementarity more generally confirmed between several items in each group

Means complementarity relationship demonstrated only between a few items in each group

AND **MEALS** WITH MEAT

Here are a selection of main dishes which use meat, but which are also rich in whole grains and legumes:

CHICKEN DIVAN CREPES

12 cooked crepes (recipe on page 86)

Filling

¼ cup butter
¼ cup flour
2 cups chicken broth
2 teaspoons Worcestershire sauce
3 cups grated cheddar cheese
2 cups sour cream of yoghurt
2 (10 oz) packages frozen broccoli, or
   1½ pounds broccoli, steamed lightly
2 cups cooked chicken

Over medium heat, melt butter in small saucepan. Stir in flour and cook until bubbly. Add broth and Worcestershire sauce; cook, stirring until thickened. Add two cups cheese. Empty sour cream into medium bowl; gradually add hot cheese sauce, stirring constantly. In large shallow baking dish place cooked broccoli and cooked chicken on each crepe. Spoon one tablespoon sauce over each. Fold crepes over. Pour remaining sauce over all. Sprinkle with remaining cup of cheese. Cover and heat in 350°F oven for 20 to 30 minutes.

BROCCOLI CASSEROLE

2 cups cream of chicken soup (recipe on page 78)
2 cups milk
¾ cup mayonnaise
1 teaspoon curry powder
2 cups grated cheddar cheese
1 large bunch broccoli, steamed just until
   bright green and sliced
1½ cups diced cooked chicken

Mix all ingredients together thoroughly. Pour into a two-quart casserole and bake in a 350°F oven about 20 minutes.

Variation: sprinkle 1 cup crushed whole wheat croutons on top before baking.

HAMBURGER STRETCHERS

My friend Frog (yep, I said Frog) has innumerable recipes for hamburger meals. While I've been staying with her and using the family computer to produce this book, I've tasted many recipe-less meals.

Here's an example which might give you the basic idea:

1 – 1½ pound ground beef
1 onion, chopped coarsely
2 stalks celery, sliced
2 #10 cans kidney beans
1 #10 can cut corn
1 #10 can tomato sauce
(Frog buys cases of canned food in bulk for lower cost and easier shopping.)

Cook beef in large skillet, draining as much fat as possible. Add onion and celery; cook until tender. Add remaining ingredients, and season with herbs and salt if you wish. Simmer ten minutes; serve over cooked brown rice.

Variations include mushrooms, parsley, mushroom soup instead of tomato sauce, chunks of canned tomatoes.

HOPPIN' JOHN

This black-eyed pea and rice meal has traditionally been served on New Year's Eve in the South.

1 cup dried black-eyed peas, soaked overnight
1 cup brown rice
4 cups water or stock
¼ pound nitrate-free bacon (frozen, in
    some supermarkets and health food stores)
1 medium onion, finely chopped
1 clove garlic, finely chopped
1 tablespoon vegetable oil
salt, pepper, parsley, and basil to taste

Combined black-eyed peas and rice in saucepan with water; bring to a boil. Reduce heat, and simmer, covered, for ½ hour. Meanwhile, broil bacon, break into small pieces, and sauté with onion and garlic in one tablespoon vegetable oil. Add to peas and rice, and simmer for another hour, or until beans are tender.

Remove from heat and add salt, pepper, parsley, and basil to taste.

CHICKEN ENCHILADAS WITH CORN AND TOFU

1 cup cooked chicken, cubed
1 large can tomato puree with tomatoes, or
1 cup stewed tomatoes and 8 ounces puree
1 can chiles
½ pound tofu,* cubed
½ – 1 cup frozen or canned corn
1 tablespoon Vigor-cup, or other
   powdered vegetable broth/seasoning
6 – 8 tortillas

Layer above ingredients in a shallow baking dish, as you would for enchiladas. Bake in a moderate oven (325-350°F) until well-heated.

HOT DOG TACOS

For some reason, little ones especially enjoy hot dogs, even when they are raised in "natural" homes! One our favorite ways to satisfy this craving is to wrap nitrate-free weiners in whole wheat tortillas.

Dubbed "hot dog tacos", this dish can include grated cheese, shredded lettuce or alfalfa sprouts, tomatoes, or whatever else you like to see in tacos or burritos. Heat the tortillas in the oven, or over a gas burner, while you warm the weiners (take them straight from the freezer, which is where these preservative-free meats should be kept).

Spread tortilla with catsup and/or other ingredients, place weiner on one edge, and roll. That's all.

HEN FRUIT FOR DINNER

The egg has become a much maligned food in recent years, yet doctors are now beginning to say that, even for those of us who must be careful about our cholesterol levels, the nutritional content of eggs is so superior that they should not be eliminated from the diet. According to nutritionist Linda Clark, studies have shown that eating as many as twelve eggs a day has not increased the cholesterol level, while other factors, such as stress, excessive smoking, and high sugar intake, have been shown to raise it.

Cholesterol is a fat-related substance which occurs naturally within our bodies, and a normal amount of it is necessary for good health. It is needed to create adrenal and sex hormones, vitamin D, and

---

*See note on page 88.

an important digestion fluid called bile. Cholesterol also is thought to play a part in lubricating the skin. Even when cholesterol-containing foods are completely eliminated, this waxy substance continues to circulate in the blood, because our bodies manufacture it.

The reason for the cholesterol scare of a decade or so ago is that when cholesterol accumulates in the arteries it seems to be related to the development of arteriosclerosis. Because cholesterol is like a fat, many doctors eliminated fats from the diets of their patients. Yet studies have shown that blood fat levels are also not reduced by the elimination of fats from the diet. A substance called lecithin, also naturally present in our bodies (and naturally contained in eggs, among other things), has a natural emulsifying effect on fat, and has been shown to decrease the cholesterol levels in some individuals.

Dr. Arthur M. Master, quoted in the *Journal of the American Medical Association*, says: "Many factors other than diet play a role in coronary disease, including emotion and behavior patterns, lack of physical exercise, excessive smoking, heredity and sex. Many nonfat nutrients appear to be involved... In the present incomplete state of our knowledge, a drastic change in the diet is not justified."

While the experts fight it out, we continue to eat eggs. Eggs are completely natural foods. They contain all the essential amino acids, making them a source of first-rate complete protein (7 or 8 grams in one large egg). In addition to the well-known cholesterol and the lesser known lecithin, eggs contain vitamins A, B2, D, and E, biotin, niacin, copper, iron, phosphorus and unsaturated fats. Egg yolks contain approximately 24 milligrams of calcium; the whites, 3 milligrams.

According to the *Nutrition Almanac*, one of my nutritional bibles, eggs should be refrigerated at all times at 45°F to 55°F to prevent the whites from becoming thin. Soiled eggs should be wiped clean with a dry cloth rather than washed, to preserve the natural protective film on the porous eggshell. What that translates to, we discovered from firsthand experience, is that if you wash your eggs, they go rotten faster. They also absorb odors and flavors faster when they have been washed.

Adelle Davis emphasized that raw eggs should not be consumed in great quantity. The *Nutrition Almanac* indicates that this is because the whites contain a protein called avidin, which interferes with the use of biotin, a B-complex vitamin. Avidin is inactivated by heat.

People who shop in health food stores often specify that they want fertile eggs. No one has ever told me why. There may be reasons to specify eggs from chickens who have not been fed hormones, or who have eaten unsprayed grain, and I personally feel that the eggs from chickens who have free range to eat a variety of bugs and grasses are far more tasty and attractive (and one would infer nutritious) than the eggs from chickens crowded into wire cages. I also think that brown eggs taste better than white eggs, but I doubt that I could substantiate that opinion.

Roll pastry fairly thin and press into a ten-inch quiche dish or 9-inch pie plate (raise height of crust by adding an extra piece around the edge if you use the pie plate). Cook onion in butter or oil until tender, add zucchini, stir, cover and remove from heat for five minutes. Drain, stir in flour and spread in pastry shell. Sprinkle with half the cheese.

Beat eggs and cream together; season as desired. Pour carefully into pastry shell. Sprinkle chopped green chiles over quiche, and arrange remaining cheese around edge of circle, surrounding center of chiles. Bake at 400°F for 15 minutes, then reduce temperature to 325°F and bake 30 minutes more. Cool for 20 minutes before slicing.

EASY AND ELEGANT CHEESE SOUFFLÉ*

    3 cups grated cheese
    4-6 slices whole wheat bread
    2 cups milk or 1½ cups milk and ½ cup wine
    3 eggs, beaten
    ½ teaspoon salt
    ½ teaspoon Worcestershire sauce
    ½ teaspoon thyme
    ½ teaspoon dry mustard
    pepper

ZESTY ZUCCHINI QUICHE

    Whole wheat pastry crust for a 9 inch pie (recipe above)
    3 to 4 cups coarsely grated zucchini (don't peel)
    1 4-ounce can whole or diced green chiles
       (remove seeds in whole chiles if you prefer a
       milder quiche, then chop finely)
    1 medium onion, sliced or chopped
    2 tablespoons butter or oil
    1 tablespoon whole wheat flour
    1 cup grated cheddar cheese
    1 cup grated Monterey Jack cheese
    3 eggs
    1 cup milk or cream

---

*From *Diet for a Small Planet*, by Frances Moore Lappe. Published by Ballantine Books.

Layer the cheese and bread in an oiled baking dish, starting with the bread. Pour over it the milk or milk mixture. Beat, with the eggs, the salt and remaining ingredients and pour this over the bread mixture also. Let stand for 30 minutes. Bake at 350°F for one hour in a pan of hot water.

WHOLE WHEAT PIE CRUST

1½ cups whole wheat pastry flour
1 teaspoon salt
½ cup butter
¼ cup ice water

Stir together flour and salt; cut in butter until texture is like coarse cornmeal. Gradually add ice water by tablespoons until pastry can be gathered together and handled easily. Chill until ready to roll.

TANGY SPINACH SOUFFLE

3 tablespoons butter
3 tablespoons whole grain flour
1 cup plain kefir or cultured buttermilk
1 medium bunch fresh spinach (enough to make about one cup of puree)
4-6 ounces sharp cheddar cheese, grated or cubed
3 eggs, separated
1 teaspoon salt
fresh pepper

Melt butter in heavy skillet over low heat. Stir in flour and cook, still stirring, for a few minutes, then gradually stir in kefir. Continue to cook over low heat, stirring frequently, until mixture comes to a boil and thickens somewhat. Stir in cheese until melted and well mixed. Put spinach into blender with one of the egg yolks to facilitate pureeing, and process until completely liquified. Add spinach mixture to pan, then stir in remaining egg yolks, stirring and cooking until yolks thicken, about another minute. Remove from heat. Season with about a teaspoon of salt and a fresh grating of pepper.

Whip egg whites until stiff but not dry; fold them lightly into vegetable mixture. Grease and flour a seven-inch souffle baker or a straight-sided baking dish, pour mixture into it, and bake for about 45 minutes, or until firm, at 350°F. Serve immediately.

DESSERTS

SUMMER SWEETS

I remember walking home from summer school one day, feeling sorry for myself, first because I had to go to school during summer vacation, and second because I didn't have enough spending money left after Girl Scout camp to stop at the Little Store and join my friends in their daily treat of twin popsicles. I also remember my delight when Mother greeted me at the door that day (was it twenty years ago?) with an ice cube made from grape juice, skewered on a toothpick.

Summer is the time of year when children and grownups alike seem to crave sweet treats more often than usual. Perhaps it is merely the warm weather, or perhaps the outside activities which take more of our physical energy coax our brains into ordering sugar. Even though we have learned that the so-called "quick energy" which comes from sweets is a myth, and that the initial rush will usually be followed by a longer tired period, still we find ourselves thinking about (and sometimes actually ordering) chocolate-covered bananas at the boardwalk, candy cotton at the fair, and slush cones at the fast food place next door to swimming lessons.

What is to be done about this recurring desire for sweet things? "I can't say 'no' all summer," complained one of my friends, "so I need a new way of phrasing it." How about "yes"? "No" is such a negative way to respond to anything, and in the hot weather it seems to turn edgy tempers into open warriors. Even when you are arguing with yourself, "no" is a bitter pill to swallow.

Here's what I mean: you are putting the kids back in the car for the fourth time that afternoon, after swim lessons, trampoline, soccer practice and the dime store, and someone pipes up "Can we have a Sloppee, Mom?"

DON'T say: "No — you can't. Sloppies have too much sugar, and artificial coloring and flavoring, besides. Wait until we get home and you can have some yoghurt and wheat germ. It's much better for you."

Does that sound like a great sales pitch for natural foods?

INSTEAD, try this: "Well, I'm ready to head for home and would rather not stop, but we can whip up some Pineapple Slushes when we get there."

You don't really have to know what a Pineapple Slush is at the time, but it helps. I've been known to promise such exotics as Cherry Delight and Freckle Floats without having any idea what they were until I started pouring ingredients into my blender.

There are some places you can go for recipes. *Natural Snacks and Treats*, by Flossie and Stan Dworkin, is a good book; so are *Taming the C.A.N.D.Y. Monster*, by Vicki Lansky, and *Natural Foods Ice Cream Book*, by Robert Soman. Once you have a feeling for what your family and friends like, however, play with the basic recipes and come up with new versions. Like a drop of vanilla or cinnamon oil in the plain yoghurt (freshly pressed flavor oils are now available in health food stores), or a grating of lemon peel on the cream cheese-spread crackers. Or blend two cups of fruit juice with two packages of unflavored gelatin and make a natural finger jello.

I use my blender a lot. A dairy product (milk, yoghurt, kefir, buttermilk, honey ice cream), some fruit (peaches, papayas, bananas, strawberries, melons), and some ice will make a thick shake. Crush just the fruit and pour it over some yoghurt or ice cream and you have a sundae. Make ice cubes out of fruit juice, crush them in a blender, add a straw, and you have a slush "cone" (more attractive to youngsters if actually served in a paper cone). Melons pureed in the blender can be frozen to form a sugarless ice.

It helps if the children, especially the older ones, make some of these things themselves. Eliminate all the recipe boks from the kitchen which were sold to you by the manufacturers of gelatin desserts and artificial whipping cream, and replace them with one or more of the fine children's natural food cookbooks that are now available. *Love at First Bite*, by Jane Cooper, or *The Fun Food Factory*, by Nanette Newman, are good choices. The illustrations are wonderful, the instructions plain, and the results delicious.

Or write the recipes for some of your (and their) favorites, and tape them to the wall by the blender, or on the refrigerator door. Make it easy to make healthy treats. Have the ingredients handy, the utensils within reach. You may find one day that your eight-year-old is talking you out of stopping for a soft drink at Hamburger Heaven because he wants to get home for his softball game, and anyway, he can whip up a Grape Ghoul for you when you get to the house!

FRESH FRUIT SUNDAE

In a tall fountain glass (available at dime stores), layer plain whole milk yoghurt and fresh sliced fruit (peaches, strawberries, cherries, etc.). Top with a layer of yoghurt, a layer of the fruit pureed in a blender, and some chopped nuts. Out-of-season fruit may be substituted by using frozen, unsweetened fruit.

If your family is not accustomed to the flavor of plain yoghurt, try sweetening it with a small amount of honey, or a teaspoon of vanilla extract per cup of yoghurt.

FRESH FRUIT GELATIN

Soak one tablespoon unflavored gelatin in ¼ cup cold water in a medium-sized bowl. Meanwhile, bring 1½ cups water to a boil and grate two fresh lemons (wash thoroughly if the lemons are commercially grown). Pour boiling water over the gelatin, stirring constantly until dissolved. Stir in ½ cup lightly flavored honey (like safflower or clover) and ¼ teaspoon salt. When gelatin and honey are completely dissolved, add the juice and grated peel of the two lemons, pour into a mold and chill thoroughly.

Other citrus fruits can be substituted by adjusting the honey and grated peel. Taste the juice before pouring it into the mold. Adding grated carrots or chopped celery turns your dessert into a salad.

Any fruit juice (except pineapple) may be made into a gelatin mold, using one package of unflavored gelatin for each two cups of juice. Bring half the juice to a boil, dissolve gelatin in it, then add other half, stir well, and chill. Grape and apple are popular choices for this treatment, but my favorite is berry juice. Check your food co-op or natural food store for unusual unsweetened juices.

"Finger jello" can be made by doubling the amount of gelatin powder used. After chilling, cut the dessert into cubes and serve on plates or in bowls. This keeps its form even at room temperature.

FRESH PEACH TAPIOCA PUDDING

3 ripe peaches, peeled, pitted, and pureed
2 eggs, separated
¼ teaspoon salt
2 tablespoons honey
vanilla-flavored yoghurt
⅓ cup small pearl tapioca

Blend together peaches, egg yolks, salt and honey. Measure, and add enough vanilla yoghurt to make three cups in all. Combine this mixture with tapioca and let stand 5 to 15 minutes. Stir thoroughly to break up any pearls which have stuck together, then cook over very low heat, stirring constantly, until fully boiling.

Continue cooking over lowest possible heat, stirring constantly to prevent sticking, for five more minutes. Remove from heat. Beat egg whites until quite stiff. Gradually stir tapioca mixture into egg whites. Cool 15 minutes before serving, or chill thoroughly. Stir again just before serving.

FROZEN BANANAS

In the summer, bananas ripen and turn brown at an amazing rate. When one or two have become too brown to appeal to the children, slice them in half crossways (peel first), and insert a popsicle stick three-quarters of its length into the cut ends. Set these on waxed paper in the freezer overnight, then wrap lightly in plastic wrap or waxed paper until ready to serve. They can be dipped in carob syrup and grated coconut, chopped nuts, or toasted wheat germ before eating, but are also delicious plain.

FRUIT FRITTERS

This sweet dish can be a meal, just right for a hot day when the lighted oven is the last thing you need in your kitchen.

4 egg yolks
1 cup plain yoghurt
½ cup cottage cheese
½ cup milk
1 cup chopped dried peaches and apricots
1 cup finely chopped diced apple
1 cup whole wheat pastry flour
½ teaspoon baking soda
½ teaspoon salt
1 teaspoon honey
4 egg whites

Cream together egg yolks, yoghurt, cheese and milk. Stir in fruit. Stir together flour, soda, salt and sugar, pressing out any lumps. Add to first mixture. Beat egg whites until stiff. Fold in. Fry in light oil at 375°F until brown. Turn, fry on other side, remove and drain. Makes about 20 three-inch fritters.

POPSICLES

Frozen fruit juice is a tasty treat for children of all ages. Either invest in a set of plastic popsicle molds, or just use paper cups and popsicle sticks, which can be purchased at craft stores.

We freeze yoghurt, also, and half-milk, half-juice combinations. Blend sparkling mineral water with fruit juice and freeze. Puree fruit, thin with juice or milk, freeze. Use your imagination.
(There are other frozen snack ideas in the Teething Treats for Toddlers section, too.)

BAKING SAMPLER

You can use whole grain flours in most of your tried and true cookie and cake recipes, if you make the adjustments gradually. Substitute one cup of whole wheat flour, for example, into a recipe calling for two or three cups of flour. Work your way up to 100% whole wheat over a six-month period, and gradually increase the leavening to accommodate the heavier flour used. Using lower-fiber whole wheat pastry flour will help you achieve a texture more like the one your family is accustomed to.

If you want to substitute honey for sugar, you can do that, too, but you can also begin by simply reducing the sugar in almost any recipe. For specific instructions for substituting honey into recipes, see the Sweeteners section.

Here are just a few examples of whole grain baked goodies:

BANANA OATMEAL COOKIES

½ cup nuts	1¾ cups rolled oats
½ cup honey	1½ cups whole wheat pastry flour
½ cup vegetable oil	1 teaspoon salt
1 egg	¼ teaspoon ground nutmeg
2 large bananas	¾ teaspoon cinnamon

Grind nuts or chop them finely. Mix honey, oil, egg, and bananas. Add to nuts and mix well. Stir together flour, salt, and spices. Combine with the rest of the ingredients to make a relatively stiff batter. If too thick to spoon out easily, add a few teaspoonfuls of fruit juice; if too thin, add more flour.

Drop by teaspoonfuls onto a lightly oiled cookie sheet. Bake at 400°F for about 15 minutes. Makes about 4 dozen.

ALMOND DROP COOKIES

2 cups whole wheat pastry flour
¼ teaspoon baking soda
¼ cup honey
1 cup butter or natural margarine
1 egg
2 teaspoons almond extract
whole almonds

Stir together flour and baking soda. Cream honey and butter, then blend in egg and almond extract. Add flour mixture to honey mixture. Shape dough into small balls and press an almond into the middle of each. Brush with beaten egg and bake on ungreased cookie sheet 15 – 20 minutes at 350°F. Makes about 6 dozen.

GINGERBREAD PEOPLE

These are a great favorite around Christmas time, but I bring out the recipe and the cookie cutters on rainy days any time of year. Good for at least an hour of entertainment!

¼ cup butter or natural margarine
¼ cup molasses (or ⅛ cup each honey
    and molasses)
1½ cup whole wheat pastry flour
¼ teaspoon salt
½ teaspoon ginger
⅛ teaspoon nutmeg
3 – 4 tablespoons water

Blend butter with warmed molasses or honey. Stir together dry ingredients and stir into butter mixture. Add water gradually until mixture can be pressed together and rolled. Chill until ready to use, then roll out ⅜ inch and cut into shapes. Bake at 325°F for 6 to 8 minutes.

CAROB NUT BROWNIES*

These are delicious brownies, rich but not too rich. Try them with yoghurt or ice cream. And if you like them less cakey, make them in a 7" x 11" or a 9" x 9" pan.

½ cup butter or oil
½ cup honey
2 eggs
½ teaspoon salt
1 teaspoon vanilla
⅓ cup carob powder
⅔ cup whole wheat flour
2 tablespoons milk powder (3½ tablespoons
    instant)
1 teaspoon baking powder
⅔ cup sunflower seeds
½ cup roasted peanuts, chopped

Cream the butter (or oil) and honey; beat in the eggs, salt, and vanilla. Stir together the carob powder, whole wheat flour, milk powder, and baking powder; blend into the creamed mixture.

Stir in the sunflower seeds and peanuts. Turn into an oiled baking pan; bake at 325°F for 20 to 25 minutes. Cool and cut into bars.

HONEY ALMOND CHEESECAKE

Crust:

½ cup graham cracker crumbs
¾ cube butter
1 teaspoon almond extract

Crush crackers; blend with butter and almond flavoring. Mix well. Press into pie dish or springform pan.

Filling:

12 ounces cream cheese   2 eggs
¼ cup light honey   1 teaspoon almond extract

Soften cheese. Blend in honey. Add eggs, almond. Beat until smooth. Bake at 350°F for 20 minutes.

---

*From *Recipes for a Small Planet*, by Ellen Buchman Ewald. Published by Ballantine Books.

TENDER CARROT CAKE

½ cup natural margarine
1 cup honey
2 eggs
¼ cup orange juice
1 teaspoon vanilla extract
2 cups grated carrots
1 cup raisins
2 cups whole wheat pastry flour
½ teaspoon salt
2 teaspoons baking powder
1 teaspoon baking soda
1½ teaspoons cinnamon
½ teaspoons each nutmeg and ginger

Cream margarine and honey together, then add eggs, orange juice and vanilla. Stir in carrots and raisins alternately with blended dry ingredients.

Turn batter into 8 x 12 inch pan, and bake 35 to 45 minutes at 350°F. When cool, ice with cream cheese blended with honey and vanilla.

BLACKBERRY APPLE PIE

Double recipe whole wheat pie crust (pg. 97)
6 green apples, peeled, cored, and sliced
3 – 4 cups blackberries, fresh, canned,
   or frozen
3 tablespoons honey
¼ cup apple juice
1 teaspoon cinnamon
4 tablespoons cornstarch

Roll out half the pie crust and fit it into a nine inch pie plate.

Stir together honey, apple juice, cinnamon and cornstarch, and blend with apples and berries in the uncooked pie crust. Roll out remaining pastry and place on top of the fruit, pinching the edges and slitting the center to allow steam to escape.

Bake the pie in a preheated 400°F oven for ten minutes, then lower the heat to 350°F and bake 30 to 40 more minutes until the crust is golden brown. Enjoy.

BEVERAGES

One day as I was searching the food co-op's refrigerator for a new selection of juices, another customer asked me how I managed to keep my children from drinking soft drinks. It seemed fairly obvious to me at the time — both of my children were preschoolers and I had total control over what they ate and drank. Yet she complained of her five-year old returning from friends' homes with cola drinks, of her seven-year old stopping after dancing lessons for slush cones at the fast food store, and of the artificially-colored powdered drink mix served each day at her three-year old's nursery school.

Until then, I had thought that outside-the-home eating wasn't generally a problem until children were eight or nine years old and had a fairly active social life. A little musing on the subject, however, and I realized that I lived in the country, where there were no fast food stores and few neighbors, and that I had repeatedly taken my children only to recreation department programs and nursery schools where the nutritional value of snacks had been considered.

Perhaps I was being naive by thinking my solution would work for others. Later, I was talking with my friend Sue, and she admitted that some of the time her children ate elsewhere and she simply had to let that happen. (Sue at the time was living in a suburban housing development.) But what, she asked me, could she serve at home which would be as tasty and popular as what they were getting on the "outside"?

Her goal was twofold. One motive, of course, was to provide healthy food within her home. Her second intention, however, was to actually compete with the soft drinks offered elsewhere, in the hope that good taste would take the place of the children's not-yet-developed good judgment.

What kinds of beverages was she trying to replace? Canned soft drinks, first of all, with their artificial color, artificial flavor, phenomenal amounts of sugar and other sweeteners, and numerous chemical additives. Also on her list of "no's" were powdered drink mixes (two tablespoons of sugar per eight-ounce glass when prepared as directed), cola drinks, which contain caffeine as well as all the other ingredients, and chocolate milk. One of Sue's main concerns was for the removal of caffeine from her children's diet, since she had noticed, as many others have, that it made them jumpy and irritable. Caffeine is contained in chocolate, cola drinks, Dr. Pepper, black tea, and, of course, coffee.

Artificial coloring and artificial flavoring have been shown to negatively affect the behavior of hyperactive children and many mothers are using the logic (which I can't fault) that perhaps these additives are not good for less sensitive children either.

Canned fruit drinks (the word "drink" is used on the label instead of "juice") are often advertised as "vitamin fortified" and are considered by many people to be a good choice for growing children, yet a glance at their labels shows them to be primarily sugar and water, with some natural fruit juice, and some synthetic, added. Artificial coloring is nearly *always* added, mostly for this generation of parents who have forgotten what real orange juice or strawberry juice look like. Soda pop is merely artificially fruit-flavored syrup, without even the ascorbic acid fortification, added to carbonated water.

So what alternatives could I offer Sue? My children may have been happy with apple/strawberry juice, and blueberry kefir, but, as Sue and others pointed out to me, "They don't know any different." (That remark was often followed by, "Just wait!")

One of the favorite drinks among my children's playmates is natural grape soda. I buy quarts or half gallons of a reasonably-priced unsweetened grape juice (read the label — frozen grape juice is usually sweetened, although at least one canner uses pear juice as a sweetener instead of sugar) and blend it, a glassful at a time, half and half with sparkling mineral water, which I also buy by the quart and cap tightly.

The same sparkle trick can be pulled with any natural fruit juice, of which there is a selection in most natural food stores. Apple-boysenberry, for example, or apricot, pomegranite, cranberry, or pineapple-coconut. Start by purchasing eight-ounce bottles for snacks to see which juices your family prefers, then order quarts by the case, and take advantage of the 10% discount most stores will give you. Cut half and half with mineral water (choose a low-priced variety), the cost is not too bad, and if you give a thought to all the dentist bills you *won't* be paying, that makes the cost even more reasonable.

Choosing unusual fruit juices once in a while provides a good variety for children, but I make a point of never running out of our staples — apple, grape-pear, and orange, all of which can be purchased in frozen form at reasonable prices from supermarkets. I said reasonable — I didn't say cheap. Compared quart for quart, the artificially flavored and colored drinks are considerably lower in price than are natural juices, but I think that buying them is a false economy. The same argument stands which I mentioned above — dentist bills and doctor bills, the inevitable results of frequent intake of large amounts of sugar, can really run up the final cost of the beverages.

In addition to fruit juices in several forms, I also regularly offer milk and water. Our water is made more special by keeping it in a container in the refrigerator. We have our own well, but tap or bottled water can be treated the same way. Water is useful for more than just brushing teeth, and children can be helped to learn that.

FRESH FRUIT SMOOTHIE

In blender container combine:

   1 cup milk or orange juice
   1 banana
   1 peach
   1 cup yoghurt or buttermilk
   1 cup ice cubes

Blend at high speed until liquid and frothy. Add honey if desired.

Change fruit combinations according to season and taste; use frozen fruit when fresh is not available.

CRANBERRY-APPLE SLUSH

Combine equal parts of cranberry juice and apple juice. Fill an ice cube tray with some of the juice; freeze. Refrigerate the rest. To serve, crush cranberry-apple cubes in blender or food processor, or pound them between layers of cloth. Place in a glass; fill glass with chilled juice.

HOT DRINKS

Tasty hot evening drinks can be made without using chocolate, tea, coffe, or sugar. We use unsweetened carob powder for our "hot chocolate", blend it with milk, vanilla, and honey, and heat it slowly, then blend it again for a foamy spicy drink. A touch of cinnamon makes it even more of a treat.

One of my favorites evolved from a form of natural "instant breakfast". For my morning drink I often combine milk, egg, milk powder, protein powder, powdered dolomite (for calcium and magnesium), lecithin (to make the drink creamy), and brewer's yeast (for B vitamins) with a piece of fruit (pulpy fruit like banana, berries, or papaya works best).

In an English train station I once enjoyed a cup of "Hot Horlicks", a malted milk mixture which is popular there. Having trouble sleeping one night back home, I heated a similar concoction. It may have been due to the calcium content of this drink, or perhaps because of its warmth, but that night I slept through thunder, lightening, and the rooster's morning song, and awakened well rested. My children enjoy it by the fire on rainy nights.

BEDTIME MALTED MILK

In a blender container combine, for each serving:

1 cup whole milk
½ cup spray-process milk powder
1 teaspoon malt powder*
½ teaspoon vanilla
1 teaspoon honey

Blend thoroughly. Heat over a low flame until nearly boiling, then return to the blender. Holding the lid on firmly, blend at high speed for one full minute. Pour into mugs, sprinkle with freshly ground ginger, nutmeg, or cinnamon, and serve. Happy dreams!

FOR GROWNUPS ONLY

Alcohol and good times have gone together for centuries and in most cultures. No matter that our temperance-minded grandmothers or our health-minded physicians have told us to take it easy on the liquor, it is a fact of life that alcoholic beverages still remain an integral part of the party scene.

Yet, have you noticed that fewer people are drinking them? I doubt that it is only happening around us and our friends, for we are (I like to think) a fairly typical group of people, but over the years more and more people have been showing up at parties with a sixpack of soft drinks instead of beer, or with a jug of apple juice instead of wine, and less and less people have been getting unpleasantly tipsy by the end of an evening of frivolity. Although I personally still enjoy my glass of wine, I applaud this new approach to celebration, and always seek to have nonalcoholic alternatives available for my guests.

---

*Malt powder is available pure, without sugar or flavorings, from some health food stores. Tell them they can get it from Giusto's Specialty Food Distributors in South San Francisco, California.

However, visiting other folks' homes has impressed me with the limited choices available even to thoughtful hosts. Although meade, fermented with honey, and wine, the grape elixer — and even beer and chicha — are relatively natural beverages, what are their nonalcoholic counterparts? Cola, made with sugar, caramel coloring, phosphoric acid and caffeine; soda pop, containing artificial coloring and flavoring, preservatives and a host of unpronounceable chemicals along with its sugar; tea or coffee, both high in caffeine; apple juice, and lemonade. During one year of office parties, barbecues, tupperware parties and beer busts, I saw no alternatives to those just listed. Apple juice and lemonade are fine, but they get a bit monotonous, don't you think?

We have always had friends among us who preferred nonalcoholic drinks, and as our gatherings seem to be including more and more children, we have collected a number of drink recipes, some of which are warm for cold evenings, others cold for hot afternoons, and which share the characteristics of being delicious and natural at the same time. You can easily do the same thing.

Look in old recipe books, or new ones for that matter, and when you see sugar or ingredients with artificial components, like soda pop, either go on to another recipe or substitute honey or fruit juice and sparkling mineral water. Many very tasty punches can be made by combining carbonated water with pure fruit juice and vanilla ice cream. Egg nogs made with real eggs and with cream and milk, sweetened with honey and spiced with cinnamon and vanilla, are far tastier, not to mention healthier and less expensive, than the prepared variety available from the dairy case.

One of our favorite nonalcoholic drinks for cold evenings, and now a regular offering for Halloween, Thanksgiving, Christmas, and New Year's Eve, is this variation on an old fashioned mulled cider.

HOLIDAY MULLED CIDER

Into a large Dutch oven or enameled canning pan, pour as much unsweetened apple juice as you feel you will need. A gallon is our minimum. Heat over a very low flame.

While it is heating, take two or three oranges and slice through the skin with a sharp knife, cutting vertically, through each end, and turning the orange a little each time, cutting six to eight times in all. Slash crosswise two or three times. Insert whole cloves at each intersection, then float the oranges in the simmering cider. Add whole allspices, two or three cinnamon sticks, a grating or four of nutmeg and a little lemon juice.

111

All of this is strictly to taste, and differs each time. We like our cider very spicy; others may prefer it milder. The spices may be combined in a square of cheesecloth tied up with string, and left in the pot as the mixture simmers, or they can be left to float in the serving cups.

This drink gets better and better, so for the fullest flavor, begin mulling early in the morning and let it simmer all day. A serving scoop left in the pot will encourage your guests to help themselves, and you will inevitably discover that you should have made more than you did.

HOT CRANBERRY MUGS

2 cups cranberry juice
¼ cup fresh orange juice
½ cup water
2-4 whole cloves
cinnamon sticks
honey

Heat liquids and cloves in a saucepan. Serve in mugs. Sweeten to taste with honey; stir with cinnamon sticks.

BLENDER EGGNOG

In a blender, combine:

1 cup milk
½ cup cream
3 egg yolks

Run the blender at low speed, and add:

¼ cup spray-process powdered milk
1 teaspoon vanilla
¼ teaspoon salt
1 tablespoon liquid lecithin (for smoothness)
1 tablespoon honey

Turn the blender to high speed and run for several minutes. Pour mixture immediately into cups and grate fresh nutmeg over each one. (Nutmegs can be purchased whole, and nutmeg graters cost less than $2.00 at specialty cookware shops. Grated fresh nutmeg is impossible to imitate.)

ICED HERBAL TEA

We make our tea with the Sun. In a quart or half-gallon jar, place fresh, cool water and two to four tea bags. My favorites have orange and spices or rose hips in them for color, but any herbal tea blend is fine. Cap jar loosely and place bottle in the sun for twenty minutes or so, until solar-induced convection circulates the tea throughout the jar. Add ice cubes and enjoy.

NATURAL "ICE CAFÉ"

Prepare a batch of hot grain beverage such as Pero, Pioneer, or Postum. Pour into tall glasses, over a scoop of vanilla ice cream (homemade, of course). Top with freshly whipped cream. Straws and tall spoons — you're done.

HOLIDAYS AND CELEBRATIONS — NEW TRADITIONS

It is becoming increasingly difficult to have a natural holiday. Last year I decided I didn't have time to make my traditional fruitcake, so started to buy a popular brand. I found my family would have been eating mono and diglycerides, polysorbate 60 and 80, artificial flavor, gum arabic, agar, artificial color, sodium benzoate, proplyene glycol, and propyl paraben along with the flour, eggs, spices, and fruit.

So I decided to buy some glaceed fruit to make a cake as usual. The label on the fruit, ignored for most of my life, listed corn syrup, sugar, artificial color, liquid dextrose, sodium benzoate, artificial flavor and sulfur dioxide.

For a few days I was stuck. Then I hit upon the idea of using plain dried fruit for our holiday cake. Candied fruit was originally marketed to substitute for the homemade product anyway, so returning to the old way might reap good results. We tried it, and were very excited with our discovery.

With the popularity of dehydrators, it seems likely that many people will have their own source of dried fruits, offsetting the cost a little (naturally dried fruit does tend to be more expensive than candied fruit).

First, though, a few words about dried fruit. The soft, brightly-colored fruit found in supermarkets has usually been treated with sulfur dioxide to prevent discoloration. Sulfur has been used since Egyptian times, when it was used to preserve wine, and except for the fact that it destroys vitamin A and leaves a bitter aftertaste, it is not particularly harmful.

If you prefer unsulfured fruit, however, as I do, dry your own or purchase it from a natural food store or co-op. In that case, you might want to rehydrate the peaches and apricots for a few minutes in boiling water before you begin cutting them, but do not soak them too long or they will become mushy.

Combine all the chopped fruit in a large bowl and dredge with flour to keep it from sticking together in lumps. After your cakes are completely cooled, you can pour brandy over them and store them wrapped in plastic wrap and aluminum foil for months or years (they improve with age). Or you can just take them out of the oven and serve, although extremely fresh fruitcake tends to crumble when sliced.

DRIED FRUIT CHRISTMAS FRUITCAKE

7 to 8 cups mixed pitted, chopped dried fruit (especially good are raisins, pears, unsweetened pineapple, apricots, cherries, apples, peaches)
1 cup chopped nuts
½ cup apple juice
1½ cups whole wheat pastry flour
1 teaspoon baking powder
1 teaspoon salt
2 teaspoons cinammon
1 teaspoon nutmeg
½ teaspoon allspice
½ pound softened butter
4 eggs
1 cup honey
¼ cup molasses

Combine chopped fruit in a large bowl; pour fruit juice over fruit and leave, covered, overnight. Dredge fruit with a few tablespoons of the flour. Stir together remainder of the flour, baking powder, salt and spices. Cream butter, eggs, honey and molasses, then stir in dry ingredients.

Fold fruit in last, then spoon into greased springform pan. Bake at 325° for 1½ hours, or until a knife inserted in the center comes out clean. Cool for 20 minutes before removing from pans.

PLUM PUDDING

An English Christmas tradition:

½ pound chopped beef suet (could be put through a meat grinder)
½ pound bread crumbs
1 cup dark honey
½ pound raisins
½ pound pitted prunes
¼ pound each chopped candied peels of citron, orange, and lemon, if available (or make your own by boiling and draining seven times, then boiling in a honey syrup for half an hour)

½ pound chopped dried or peeled fresh apples
grated rind of a lemon
½ cup whole wheat pastry flour
½ teaspoon grated cinnamon
½ teaspoon mace
1 teaspoon nutmeg
½ teaspoon cloves
1 teaspoon salt
½ cup cider, fruit juice, brandy or sherry
6 eggs, separated

Dredge the suet and fruit in the combined flour and seasonings, blending with your hands to separate all the sticky pieces. Add honey, liquid, crumbs, and well-beaten egg yolks. Stir well. This can be mixed, except for the eggs, a week or two before needed, and stirred daily (for good luck, have each member of the household stir at least once).

Just before steaming, beat the egg whites until stiff and fold gently into the mixture. Wrap in a strong cloth which has been wet, buttered, and floured. Place in a saucepan of boiling water (leave a little room for the pudding to swell). Cover pan and boil for six hours, adding boiling water as needed. Let stand for 15 minutes before unmolding. Decorate with holly and ivy, lace with brandy, ignite, and serve with the following custard sauce.

CUSTARD SAUCE

2 cups milk
2 tablespoons cornstarch or arrowroot powder
2 tablespoons honey
2 well-beaten eggs
1 teaspoon vanilla

Bring all but ¼ cup of the milk to a boil. While it is heating, stir remaining milk into cornstarch in a 1 quart measuring cup or medium-sized bowl. Pour hot milk into cornstarch mixture, stir well, add honey and return to pan. Return to the boil, then pour once more into serving container which contains well beaten eggs. Stir in vanilla. Cool slightly and serve over pudding or stewed fruit.

For thicker pudding, return mixture to pan after stirring into eggs, and return to boil before adding vanilla.

Since giving more of our attention to Christmas traditions, we have discovered that with each of our holidays we have added some traditional foods to our modern meals. They weave a thread of continuity through our otherwise crazy life, and I highly recommend that you try some of them.

PUMPKIN NUT BREAD

A Thanksgiving favorite.

 2 cups fresh cooked pumpkin
 ½ cup honey
 ½ cup vegetable oil
 2¾ cups whole wheat flour
 1 teaspoon cinnamon
 2 teaspoons baking powder
 2 teaspoons ground cloves
 ½ cup chopped nuts

Drain cooked pumpkin thoroughly in a sieve, then combine with honey and oil. Stir together flour, spices, and baking powder, pressing out any lumps. Add nuts.

Add to first mixture and pour batter into well-greased tin cans (soup cans work well), filling each can ⅔ full. Bake at 350° for 45 to 60 minutes, or until a cake tester comes out clean. Cool slightly before removing from cans and slicing. This slices best when it has been refrigerated overnight.

HOT CROSS BUNS: A Traditional Easter Treat

 2 tablespoons active dry yeast
 2 tablespoons honey
 ½ cup lukewarm milk
 3½ – 4½ cups whole wheat pastry flour
 ½ teaspoon salt
 1 teaspoon ground allspice
 1 teaspoon ground cinnamon
 2 eggs
 4 tablespoons softened butter
 ¾ cup raisins or currants
 1 lightly beaten egg

Stir together honey, yeast, and milk. Let stand in bowl for about five minutes, until bubbly. Beat in eggs, butter and raisins. Stir together flour, salt and spices, reserving about ½ cup of flour to add during kneading. Add to liquid.

Stir until blended, kneading in remaining flour until as much flour as can be absorbed easily has been blended into the dough, which should be pliable. Knead well for ten minutes. L rise, covered, in a bowl in a warm place, for about 45 minutes.

Make about 24 balls out of the dough. Arrange them about 2 inches apart on a well-buttered baking sheet, then leave, in a warm place, covered with a towel, to rise for about 15 or 20 minutes.

Cut a cross in the top of each one with a sharp knife. Brush lightly with beaten egg and bake in the middle of the oven 450°F for about 15 minutes. Cool slightly before removing from pans. Crosses can also be decorated with strips of dough or honeyed orange peel. Serve hot.

INDIAN PUDDING

Versions of this recipe date from the first Thanksgiving. It was named Indian Pudding by the colonists, not because the recipe came from the Indians, but because it is made with cornmeal, known then as Indian meal. Be sure that your cornmeal is made from whole grain corn, and does not say "degerminated" on the container (that means the corn germ has been removed).

½ cup whole cornmeal
¼ teaspoon salt
¼ teaspoon baking soda
1½ cups milk
2 tablespoons butter
1 egg, beaten
¼ cup blackstrap molasses
¼ cup light honey
1 teaspoon ground cinnamon
½ teaspoon grated nutmeg
½ teaspoon ground ginger
1 cup heavy cream

Combine cornmeal, salt, milk, and butter in medium saucepan. Bring to boil, stirring constantly, and remove from heat. Combine egg, honey, molasses, honey, spices and baking soda (press out any lumps in soda with back of spoon); stir into cornmeal mixture. Pour into ungreased one-quart baking dish. Bake uncovered at 325°F for about 1½ hours, or until tip of knife inserted one inch from center of pudding comes out clean. Serve pudding warm with thick cream.

EASTER EGG BREAD

12 colored hard-cooked eggs (to color, we use onion skins tied on eggs with strings during cooking) Refrigerate eggs until last kneading.

½ cup milk
½ cup honey
1 teaspoon salt
½ cup butter
grated peel of two lemons
2 tablespoons active dry yeast (2 pkgs)
¼ cup warm water
2 eggs, beaten
4½ – 5 cups whole wheat flour
1 beaten egg
poppy seeds

Combine milk, honey, salt, butter and lemon peel — heat in pan just until butter begins to melt. Cool to lukewarm. Meanwhile, dissolve yeast in warm water, preferably in the same container which was used to measure the honey (that gives the yeast some food and gets it growing faster). Add to milk mixture after about five minutes, along with the eggs and half of the flour. Beat until smooth.

Stir in enough remaining flour, a little at a time, to form a dough you can handle with floured hands. Continue to add flour, kneading thoroughly until smooth and elastic. Place into a slightly greased bowl, cover with a cloth, and allow to rise until doubled in bulk; about one hour. Punch down and form into four long ropes. Twist the ropes together, two at a time, to form loose braids on a cookie sheet, bringing the ends together to form a ring, and nestle six colored eggs in the loops made. Or form twelve dough circles, with one egg in each circle.

Allow dough to rise again until doubled, covered with a cloth to keep out drafts and passing children. Brush dough with a beaten egg; sprinkle with poppy seeds or finely slivered almonds. Bake for 25 or 30 minutes at 375°F,; about 20 minutes for individual rings. Serve warm.

This bread can be personalized by the addition of raisins, currants, nuts, etc., and can also be made the night before and heated before serving. Enjoy.

CHALLAH (JEWISH EGG BRAID)

2 tablespons active dry yeast
1½ cups lukewarm water
2 tablespoons honey
1 egg
1 tablespoon vegetable oil
½ teaspoon salt
5-6 cups whole wheat flour

Dissolve yeast in the water, to which the honey may be added. Stir in egg, oil, salt, and half of the flour and beat until gluten is developed. Add remaining flour, more or less until dough is of the right consistency to be kneaded. Knead thoroughly, then set in oil bowl, covered with a cloth, for about 45 minutes, until doubled in bulk. Punch down, knead briefly, and divide into three parts. Roll each part into a long rope, lay ropes across each other at the center, and braid from the center out to each end. Pinch ends and place braid on a buttered baking sheet or in a long loaf pan. Cover and let rise again until doubled. Brush with milk or a beaten egg yolk and sprinkle with poppy seeds. Bake 50 to 60 minutes at 375°F.

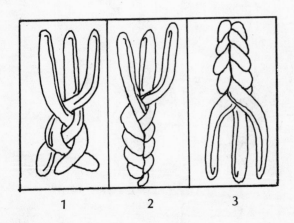

1   2   3

GROWING IN YOUR KITCHEN

Organic cooking, just like any other kind of cooking, can be a daily chore, just something we have to do to get the food on the table, or it can be a challenge, a project we look forward to and enjoy completing. The topics in this chapter are primarily of that latter type — odds and ends of interesting ways to cook things "from scratch" which are certainly not necessary for a healthy family, but which some cooks might find enjoyable.

All of the items covered here can be purchased in most large natural food stores and supermarkets. Some of them are even less expensive when purchased than they are when prepared at home. However, all are worth, I think, a weekend's experiment at least once, and more than one of them may catch your interest and push you to a new growth in your kitchen skills. I hope so.

LET'S HAVE A LITTLE CULTURE

"Yoghurt – yuk!" How often have you heard someone say that? Probably less often since frozen yoghurt made its debut and lots of money has been spent promoting it, and since a few leading magazines have recently worked elegant desserts and salads around this tangy substance, but still, often enough that I feel I must give yoghurt a few supportive words.

Why? Well, at least partly because yoghurt and I have become friends over the years, and because I am thoroughly aware that it is an acquired taste, and also because I think it is a superior food which is neglected too often in Western diets.

I first met yoghurt when I worked in an electronics research firm, and began eating out of those awful machines that large companies often use to substitute for a cafeteria. Ours was stocked by a more thoughtful vendor than some, however, for it generally contained hard-boiled eggs, fresh fruit, and yoghurt along with the chicken salad sandwiches on white bread and the small cans of chili beans.

I was watching my weight (I'm *always* watching my weight, not that it does much good), and yoghurt had always seemed like a diet food to me, so I began buying a cup of it each day for lunch. I ate more sweet foods then than I do now, and I found it very difficult at first to manage the almost bitter flavor which the plain yoghurt presented to me, so usually chose a fruit variety to help me get it down.

As my tastes matured through the years, I began making my own yoghurt at home and flavoring it with fresh fruit and honey, then with only fresh fruit (sometimes pureed in my blender), and now more often than not I just top a dollop of plain yoghurt with a little wheat germ or sesame seeds and eat it as is.

Once you acquire the taste of plain yoghurt you may find that the pre-flavored and sweetened ones are no longer interesting. That is the time to explore the delicious fruit yoghurts now becoming available at supermarkets and health food stores which have plain yoghurt on the top and honey-sweetened fruit at the bottom. There are now a number of brands available now with no artificial colorings, and some are quite tasty.

Yoghurt and its related milk cultures, kefir, buttermilk, and cheese, are not traditional Western foods. Fermented milk products, which all of these are, have been made in the homes and used in daily cooking for thousands of years in places like Turkey, Bulgaria, and India, and a look at the variety of recipes using them indicates that yoghurt is used there as a staple, not as a specialty food, as it is in the U.S.

Many people cannot in their adulthood digest sweet milk. According to Beatrice Trum Hunter (author of Yoghurt, Kefir, and Other Milk Cultures), this is due to the gradual reduction of an enzyme, lactase, which is used by the body to break down milk sugar, or lactose, and utilize it. Almost all infants have a high level of lactase, but after weaning, produce less of this enzyme, and in some adults the production is so minimal that milk digestion is almost impossible.

Someone with a lactose intolerance will suffer abdominal cramps, gas, and diarrhea, and will begin to shy away from milk entirely. It could be that there is no harm in this — some people point out that no other mammal consumes milk beyond infancy — yet the nutritional benefits of milk are significant. Perhaps switching to fermented milk products is the answer for those people who have difficulty with sweet milk, because these products are low in lactose.

Beatrice Trum Hunter also reports research findings indicating relief from many gastrointestinal disorders by the regular consumption of fermented milk; the addition of yoghurt and kefir to a diet has been shown to improve the appetite, aid digestion, and encourage healing of peptic ulcers, gastroenteritis, colitis, diarrhea and dysentery.

Knowing doctors now prescribe yoghurt along with their anti-biotics, because the bacteria present in yoghurt, *Lactobacillus bulgaricus*, grow in the intestinal tract to help replace the bacteria normally present there and destroyed by the antibiotics. More valuable even than *L. bulgaricus* is *L. acidophilus*, present in some yoghurt cultures (read the label), and in kefir, a cultured milk product similar to yoghurt in its tanginess, but in liquid form. Kefir is available in half-pints and quarts in most health food stores, and is the best defense against stomach disorders I have ever found.

If you begin slowly with yoghurt and kefir products, working them into your cooking and snacking, I am sure you will discover yourself acquiring the taste to the point of wanting to make your own. Excellent yoghurt and kefir starters are available from health food stores, containing satisfactory instructions for the beginner. In addition, there are numerous books on the subject of milk culture and a whole collection of people already growing their own, so to speak. Ask around. You'll be surprised to find who among your friends secretly has been a closet yoghurt fan.

Making your own yoghurt is a lot like baking bread; the results vary depending upon the humidity, the temperature, and (probably) the phases of the moon. Still, there are some tricks to getting your yoghurt to turn out right.

Look at the selection of yoghurt in your natural food store dairy case the next time you are there. Read the labels. You will see, repeatedly, ingredients such as nonfat milk solids, agar, gelatine, dairy whey, and even cream. If you make yoghurt according to most instructions you find in most recipe books or on packets of yoghurt starter, you will not be including any of these things. And if your first yoghurt also turns out runny and thin, perhaps that is why. Perhaps you should add some kind of thickener like the big guys do.

Yoghurt as it is made in the Middle East and Eastern Europe is often not the firm custardy texture we have come to expect in the U.S. It is frequently so tender you can drink it, and so tart the Western palate has to work to develop a liking for it.

Some of the runniness in Eastern yoghurts is due to the lower fat content of goat and other milks which are used. Adelle Davis (in *Let's Cook It Right*) attributes some of the total refusals to set in home made yoghurt, however, to penicillin or other antibiotics contained in the milk obtained from commercial dairies. The authors of *Laurel's Kitchen* warn us never to use yoghurt containing stabilizers for starter, to always sterilize yoghurt-making equipment, and to never use instant powdered milk unless it is spray-processed.

Following those precautions, then, here is a recipe you can try. When I make yoghurt I like to use raw milk, boiled to remove the enzymes which, although good for me, destroy yoghurt bacteria. You may use pasteurized milk, however, and obtain results which are just as satisfactory.

To one quart of raw or pasteurized milk (or use one cup milk powder blended in one quart water) placed in a blender container, add ¼ cup spray-process powdered milk. Blend until the powder is thoroughly dissolved. Heat this mixture slowly to boiling (omit this step if using only powdered milk), and boil for at least 15 seconds. Cool to lukewarm — maximum temperature 115°F.

If you are making your yoghurt in several small containers, put about a teaspoon of yoghurt from a previous batch, or from a

126

commercial type, into each container, then pour the milk mixture over it and stir to blend. If you make your yoghurt in a quart jar, one or two tablespoons of yoghurt starter will be enough.

Keep your containers at the magic temperature, between 100°F and 120°F (I don't like to go over 115° — the lower temperature may slow the thickening, but at least it won't kill the bacteria), until thick. I've never had a batch thicken in less than five hours, and sometimes it takes as long as 10 or 12.

Things I have noticed: If you leave your yoghurt in its warm place too long, or don't chill it thoroughly right after it thickens, it tends to separate. Separation won't really hurt it, but it doesn't look very pretty.

More is not necessarily better: I find that ¼ cup of powdered milk to a quart of regular milk is just about right. Any more powder, and it begins to taste chalky.

Sometimes yoghurt makers do break down: If you get consistently runny yoghurt from one or two jars, consider that the heating element may be going crazy.

If at first homemade yoghurt is too tangy for you to eat plain, try using part evaporated milk in your next batch. Another thing you can try is to add a few drops of vanilla extract, or a scant drop of one of the new flavor oils available at health food stores. A teaspoon of apple concentrate turns a cup of plain yoghurt into a dessert; a spoonful of fresh fruit puree will make a treat that most children will like. Any flavorings or fruit should added after the yoghurt is set.

If you still get a batch of runny yoghurt now and again, don't throw it out. Use it as you would buttermilk — make salad dressing out of it, put it into pancakes or bread, or just add flavorings and drink it. You can use properly set yoghurt wherever you would use sour or sweet cream — in salad dressings, over fruit or pancakes, in stroganoff. When you begin making your own yoghurt, and find that you constantly have some on hand, it will cease to be an occasional treat and begin to be a frequently used ingredient.

CHEESE IS A NATURAL FOOD — OR IS IT?

Cheese is one of our staple foods. When the children are looking for a snack between meals, a chunk of cheese is often the solution; if I am in the middle of a chapter and don't want to stop, a large wedge of cheese becomes my lunch. In the morning, cheese is crumbled into the omelet; at noon it is cubed and added to the soup; at dinner, it is grated to dress up the vegetable. Special dinners often highlight a cheese fondue; an extra guest may result in a cheese souffle; an unplanned delay before dinner might be filled with cheese cubes served on toothpicks.

But cheese is cheese, right? Wrong. Some cheeses have preservatives added, some have been artificially colored, and some have been blended, homogenized, emulsified and pasteurized to produce a predictable, repeatable, plastic product.

Start reading cheese labels. If you see orange, think "coloring". Cheese is naturally white or very pale yellow, never orange. If you cannot find the original labels due to repackaging, go to a cheese shop and buy fresh wedges from the original wheel, and read the labels there. Some brands of cheese consistently use preservatives and colorings; others have a line of natural cheeses and another line of commercial.

One of the saddest products we as a nation have sent out into the world is American cheese. By that I don't mean the entire American cheese industry, but the processed plastic stuff which has become known as American Cheese — the stuff Snoopy said the moon was made out of. In addition to the bad things that have been done to the texture, the color, and the fragrance, the flavor of American processed cheese is insipid. Once we became accustomed to the variations in fragrance, texture, and flavor of European and more traditional Domestic cheeses, American Cheese became a stranger to our home.

Milk used for making cheese in the U.S. must, by law, be pasteurized, or else the ensuing cheese must be aged for thirty days to ensure the death of harmful bacteria. If you have never eaten cheese made from raw milk, you have a treat ahead of you. Cooking the milk reduces the flavor of the cheese, and aged cheese has been considered safer than fresh cheese for centuries, so aged raw milk cheese gives you the best of both worlds.

In other countries cheese is usually stronger in flavor than in America. This is partly because pasteurization is not required, and partly because milks from differing areas and from cows with differing diets are curdled and combined, resulting in many wonderful flavors. Unfortunately for the cheese lover, imported cheeses must conform to

128

our pasteurized milk requirement, the only exceptions being some of the aged cheeses, so our choices are limited.

Start looking more carefully at cheese. Try different types; use them in different ways. Try to avoid processed cheeses, or any which have had coloring or preservatives added. Properly made cheese does not need crutches like preservatives or pasteurization to be safe, and the flavors are incredible when the cheesemakers do their stuff unhampered. If you get really inspired, you might even want to try making your own cheese.

Making cheese has been one of my greatest adventures in the kitchen. Regular cheesemaking at home is probably only feasible if you have your own cow or goat, since you only get a pound of cheese from five or six quarts of milk, which would be expensive if you were buying pasteurized milk from the market. However, making it once in a while can be fun, and helps you and your family to understand the process. After making cheese in one of my classes last winter, several people remarked that they would never again complain about the price of cheese!

Cheesemaking is not difficult, but it does take a chunk of time and several pieces of equipment. Since it takes a lot of milk, and a lot of time, it would be disappointing to have a batch fail, so be sure that you have a good set of instructions before you begin.

Rather than trying to condense an entire chapter or book into the space allowed here for the subject, I am instead going to give you some good references and let you read the directions in their entirety. There are many cheesemaking books and recipes being published in these days of "return to the simple life".

Three excellent sources are: *Stocking Up: How to Preserve the Foods You Grow, Naturally*, by The Editors of Organic Gardening and Farming, Rodale Press; *Old Fashioned Recipe Book*, by Carla Emery; and *The Super-Easy Step-by-Step Cheese-Making Book*, by Yvonne Young Tarr.

TOFU AND SOYMILK

Tofu is a cheeselike food which is made from soymilk. Soymilk is a liquid which is made from dried soy beans. Soymilk can be a wonderful milk substitute for the child who is beyond breast milk, yet shows one of the allergies or intolerances often linked with cow's milk, and it is a flavorful and useful liquid protein which can be used in many ways.

Tofu is probably already known to you as the white cubes in most Oriental soups. It is an extremely rich form of soy protein, and can be served in many ways, both as a meat extender and in its own right. Tofu and soymilk are really useful for the child who is either too young to serve eggs and cheese, or who for some reason won't or cannot eat them. A common question is "How in the heck do I get protein into this kid?" Here's a fine way.

Tofu is available in many supermarkets. You'll find it with the Oriental vegetables or in the cheese or delicatessen case, as it needs to be kept refrigerated. Learn the delivery days; purchased fresh and sweetened with fresh water each day, tofu will keep for three to five days in your refrigerator.

If for some reason you cannot find tofu, you might prefer to make it yourself. Like making cheese, preparing tofu is a time-consuming project (40-60 minutes) which dirties many pieces of kitchen equipment. Unlike making cheese, however, making tofu saves you money. You can make a pound of tofu from about ten cents worth of soybeans, while the retail prices varies from $.69 to $1.50.

Although making tofu is not difficult, it does take a clear and fairly extensive set of directions in order to help you keep your utensils sorted out and your kitchen in order. These directions are printed in their entirety in my book, *The Book of Whole Grains*, and of course also in *The Book of Tofu*, by William Shurtleff and Akiko Aoyagi, which was my original source. I suggest that you obtain one of these books and give tofu-making a try. We found it to be a lot of fun, and almost magical, just like cheese-making, when the curds firmed and solidified into a block. Homemade tofu also tastes better than the kind you can buy in a store. I hope you decide to try it.

HOMEMADE SOYMILK (from Whole Soybeans)*

This delicious soymilk contains about 3.7 percent protein (vs 3.3 for dairy milk) and takes only 20 minutes to prepare.

The necessary utensils are found in any typical kitchen. A stainless or glass blender are ideal. If using a plastic blender bowl that will not stand boiling water, or a food mill or juicer, see Variation 1, below. To make silken tofu or yuba, use the rich soymilk described at Variation 2. Note: do *not* use soybeans that are more than one year old; they yield a starchy thick milk that clogs the pressing sack.

To make 2 quarts soymilk:

> 1½ cups dry soybeans, washed and drained 3 times, soaked
>   in 4 to 6 cups water at room temperature for about 10
>   hours, then drained and rinsed well
> 12 cups hot water

1) Bring 12 cups water to a boil. Place a deep 6-to-8-quart cooking pot in sink, set a large colander in mouth of pot, and line colander with a moistened "pressing sack" 15 inches wide and 15 inches deep made of coarse-weave linen (Marlene's note: cheesecloth works well). Divide soaked beans into three equal portions, about 1⅓ cups each.

2) Preheat a glass, stainless steel, or heatproof plastic blender bowl by slowly pouring in 2 to 3 cups boiling water, allowing it to stand for 1 minute, then discarding water. Combine one portion of beans with 2 cups boiling water from teapot in blender and puree at high speed for 1 minute, or until very smooth. Pour puree into sack in colander. Puree remaining portions of beans with 2 cups water each and pour into sack. Rinse out blender with ¼ cup boiling water to retrieve any puree and pour into sack.

3) Twist closed mouth of sack. Using a glass jar or potato masher, press sack repeatedly against bottom of colander to extract as much soymilk as possible. Shake mouth of sack wide in colander, stir okara briefly, then pour 2½ cups boiling water over okara. Stir again, twist closed sack, and again press repeatedly with jar. Transfer cooking pot containing soymilk to stove. Reserve okara for use in cooking. (Or to get ½ cup more soymilk, open sack wide, allow okara to cool for 5 minutes, then twist closed sack and use your hands to squeeze out remaining soymilk.)

---

*Used with permission of New-Age Foods Study Center, P.O. Box 234, Lafayette, CA 94549

4) Bring soymilk to a boil over medium-high heat, stirring bottom of cooking pot constantly with a wooden spatula or spoon to prevent sticking. When foam suddenly rises in pot (or milk comes to a boil) reduce heat to medium and simmer for 7 minutes, then remove pot from burner. (Or heat for 30 minutes in a covered double boiler or in a covered saucepan set in a pot of boiling water.)

If desired, add to the 7½ cups soymilk one of the following popular flavoring combinations, listed with our favorites first:

Honey Vanilla Soymilk: Add 2½ to 4 tablespoons honey or natural sugar, ¼ teaspoon or less vanilla extract, and a pinch of salt; mix or puree well.

Rich and Creamy Soymilk: To any of the flavoring combinations above or below, add 2 to 3 tablespoons vegetable oil; puree at high speed until well dispersed. For extra thickness, add ¼ teaspoon granular lecithin.

Carob-Honey Soymilk: Add 4 tablespoons honey or natural sugar, a pinch of salt and, if desired, ¼ teaspoon vanilla extract. *After* milk has cooled, whip in 2½ to 4 teaspoons carob (or cocoa) powder, which has first been creamed in a little of the cold milk.

Malt, Mocha, or Coffee Soymilk: Add 2 to 3 tablespoons granular malt, mocha, or coffee to the Honey-Vanilla Soymilk, above.

Sesame or Calcium-Rich Soymilk: To Honey-Vanilla or Rich & Creamy Soymilk, add 5 to 8 tablespoons sesame butter, a rich calcium source (or cool milk and add 1 teaspoon calcium lactate).

Orange Soymilk: Stir 1¼ cups orange juice into cold soymilk.

Other Flavorings: Try strawberry, grated gingerroot, cinnamon and anise, nut butters, egg yolk or whole egg, butter, or coconut.

5) Soymilk may now be served hot. Or, for a richer, creamier consistency, a deeper natural sweetness, and a flavor more like that of dairy milk, chill by covering pot and setting it in circulating cold water for 10 to 15 minutes; this quick cooling increases shelf life. Pour soymilk into clean (or sterilized) bottles and cover tightly. Refrigerated, it will keep for 3 to 6 days; frozen, indefinitely.

VARIATIONS

1. Non-boiling Water Grind: If using a plastic blender that will not stand boiling water, substitute hottest tap water when pureeing, but

mix okara with boiling water. If using a food mill or juicer, grind beans without water, mix ground beans with 6 cups boiling water, and allow to stand for 2 to 3 minutes. Rinse out mill or juicer with ¼ cup boiling water, then transfer puree to pressing sack and proceed from Step 3.

2. Rich Homemade Soymilk (makes 3¼ cups): Soak only 1 cup dry soybeans. Drain, divide into 2 equal portions, and puree each portion with 1¾ cups boiling water. Rinse blender with ¼ cup boiling water, extract soymilk in pressing sack, then sprinkle okara with ½ cup boiling water and re-press. Use to make silken tofu, soft tofu, or yuba, or like cream in cookery.

3. High-yielding Soymilk: In Step 3, rinse okara with 3½ to 4½ cups boiling water. Yields 8½ to 9½ cups thinner (but still good) soymilk.

SPROUTING OUT

Growing sprouted seeds is one way to have a vegetable garden all year, and to have everyone in the family participate in growing their own food. We use sprouts in sandwiches, soups, salads, and for munching, and they provide a tasty and nutritious change from other greens, as well as a base for salads in the months when lettuce prices soar.

Natural food stores and co-ops now carry a wide range of seeds which have been germination tested and certified to be free of sprays and other toxic chemicals, and a small selection of these should start your sprouting venture with lots of material for experiments.

I usually sprout seeds in a simple wide-mouth quart jar. For years I merely placed a square of cheesecloth over the jar and screwed a canning rim over it; now I use a commercial set of plastic lids which have three different sizes of holes in them, permitting the most efficient removal of water for the least loss in seeds. Check kitchenware sections of department stores for these and for the several other types of sprouters which are now available — or use the quart jar arrangement I started with; it works fine.

Soak your seeds overnight first. Use from a tablespoon to ¼ cup at a time, depending upon the size of your container and the size of your family. A tablespoon of alfalfa seeds will sprout to fill a quart jar in three or four days; ¼ cup grows to the capacity of a gallon jar.

The initial soaking gets the seeds nice and water-engorged and starts the shell to splitting. Sometimes the first signs of sprouting shoots will be visible by the time you are ready to wash the seeds. Pour off the liquid (use it to make soup or water plants), rinse the seeds thoroughly, then set the jar or other container where the seeds can drain.

Most books about sprouting recommend placing the sprouting seeds in a dark cupboard, since too much heat and light can either dry out the seeds or promote the growth of mold. If your kitchen has a shady spot, that might work better. I find that if I put the jar away inside a closet, I forget to rinse it several times a day, which is also important for the prevention of mold growth.

Rinse the seeds several times a day for two or three days. Small seeds will now be ready to eat, although larger seeds take a little longer. If you are away from home during the day, keep the sprouts in a cool place and rinse morning and evening. Except for the hottest part of the summer, that works fairly well.

If you've kept the sprouting seeds away from the light during this part of their growth, place them in a sunny windowsill for a few hours to soak up the chlorophyll from old Mr. Sun and to increase their Vitamin C content.

Many different kinds of seeds can be sprouted, from alfalfa, clover, and radish, to wheat, oats, mung beans, lentils, and soybeans. Two precautions, however, should always be observed when sprouting:

(1) Be *absolutely sure* that the seeds you use are certified to be free of chemicals. Many seeds sold for planting have been treated with fungicides, insecticides or methyl dyes, and these should not be used for sprouting, as many of them are extremely toxic. Seeds and beans which are safe for sprouting are often available from supermarkets, health food stores, plant nurseries, and mail-order seed companies (specify that the seeds are to be used for sprouting, not planting). In some cases you might find it easiest to grow your own.

(2) Do not sprout tomato seeds or potatoes — these sprouts are *highly poisonous*. Other seeds to avoid are tree fruits, sorghum and Sudan grass.

BREAD BAKING

Baking your own bread can be a wonderfully satisfying project, netting tasty fresh loaves of nutritious whole grains and a feeling of smug satisfaction, or it can be a pain in the neck and not worth the trouble. A lot of the decision to bake or not to bake your daily bread will be influenced by your personality, the number and age of your children, and your living circumstances.

When I was first cooking for John and myself, and we had no children, making bread was a once-in-a-while project which was just plain fun. It netted us two or three loaves of bread to share with friends, or hot French bread for a company dinner, and we generally ate it all at one sitting, remarked on its quality (or lack of it), and forgot it. We only ate a loaf or two of bread a week for sandwiches, toast, and such, and bread was not really even considered a staple.

After each child was born, bread baking disappeared for a time, seeming like simply too much trouble. However, after each little one was big enough to sit and watch from a high chair or stool, and then to help, it gradually became a weekly project which exercised my arms and my psyche and made me feel good. I often made a double batch and froze part of it — extra mouths to feed on short notice were never a problem that way, and snacking on peanut butter sandwiches lost some of its sinfulness when I realized that it was on good whole grain bread.

We've had poor times, when making our own bread was the only way we could afford nutritious loaves, and busy times, when I had to stay up until midnight to squeeze in the baking. We've also had times when the bread simply didn't get made, but we found we were able to make do, now that the grocery stores often carry good firm bread without preservatives.

In other words, baking bread shouldn't be a duty, but rather a pleasure. You can help cut costs, you can make sure that you're eating nutritious bread, and you can enjoy yourself, all at once, but there's absolutely no reason to make baking bread into a martyr trip.

You can buy excellent bread now in most supermarkets. Read the label. Try to get bread which has whole wheat flour (not "wheat flour" "enriched flour", or "unbleached flour") as the first ingredient, and which does not contain BHA, BHT, or other chemical preservatives. Try to get one which contains molasses, honey, or raisin syrup instead of refined sugar. And test several types until you find bread which satisfies both your desire for wholesome bread and also your family's tastes. Otherwise it won't be eaten, and it does no good at all in the refrigerator. Yes, do keep whole grain products in the refrigerator — they contain the entire germ of wheat, including the volatile oils, and they can easily become rancid. Treat them like the living organisms they are.

If you do decide to enter the world of bread baking, I refer you to *Baking Your Own Bread*, by Nikki and David Goldbeck, or to the section in my own book, *The Book of Whole Grains*, entitled "Some Thoughts on Bread Baking". It helps to know someone who bakes her (or his) own bread to give you some "hands on" experience with kneading to help you know what it should feel like, but it's possible to do it on your own. Read a little, then give it a try. I think you'll be glad you did.

BASIC WHOLE GRAIN BREAD

3 cups liquid
3 tablespoons oil or other fat
1 tablespoon salt
½ cup honey
2 tablespoon active dry yeast (always read labels; some contain preservatives)
¼ cup lukewarm water
7 – 8 cups whole wheat flour (1 cup gluten flour improves rising and texture)

Combine liquid, fat, salt, and honey in saucepan or large bowl (it helps to heat to dissolve fat, salt and honey), and cool to lukewarm. Liquid can be water, milk, soup stock, fruit juice, or a combination of those things.

Dissolve yeast in ¼ cup lukewarm water (use the same cup used for measuring honey and it will give the yeast a bubbly start); when activated, add to mixture in bowl. Stir in 3 – 4 cups flour, beating well to develop gluten.

Stir in remaining flour (add raisins, grits, or other nongluten-containing ingredients at this point), and beat as long as you can, then turn onto floured board. Add more flour if necessary to obtain a workable dough. Knead thoroughly until dough is smooth and elastic.

Turn dough into oiled bowl, revolving once to coat. Cover with a damp cloth and let it rise in a warm place for about an hour. Punch down, form into two loaves, and place in well-greased bread tins. Let rise, covered, 45 minutes. Bake at 375°F for 45 minutes, or until the loaf sounds hollow when thumped. Remove from bread tins and cool on racks. Cool thoroughly before slicing.

VARIATIONS

1. Use tomato juice and water, half and half; add 1 cup grated cheese. Omit honey.

2. Use 1 cup cooked cereal or cracked wheat, softened in 2 cups hot water (count as part of the 3 cups liquid), in place of ¾ cup flour. Add ½ cup powdered milk.

3. Substitute 1 cup soy grits or flakes, softened in 2 cups hot water as in #2.

4. Use 1 cup nine grain cereal for 1 cup flour. Add 1 cup of raisins; use maple syrup instead of honey; use milk for the liquid.

5. One cup oatmeal instead of 1 cup flour. Add a beaten egg.

6. Make with ½ white flour, ½ whole wheat. Add 1 cup of wheat germ. Good starter for a family unaccustomed to whole grains.

7. Herb bread: ½ cup grated zucchini and ½ cup grated carrot. One tablespoon each of oregano, basil, dill, marjoram.

8. Add ½ cup molasses; use ½ cup carob flour for ½ cup of flour.

HOMEMADE CRACKERS

Homemade crackers never used to be much of a success around our house. Intellectually, I have always felt that if something is made at home, from whole and natural ingredients, it must be superior to anything a breakfast cereal conglomerate has to offer. Yet emotionally, biting into one of my own creations never seemed to be quite so satisfying as a handful of Rye Crisps or Triscuits.

Since I long ago learned to live with that knowledge, how could I argue when my family placed boxes of commercial crackers into my grocery cart? I tackled the labels immediately, and vetoed everything with preservatives and artificial coloring, but beyond that I usually succumbed, leaving us with a dismal succession of one whole grain cracker after another.

For the other fact that I learned to live with is that there is very little variety in store bought whole grain crackers. They spoil quickly, since they have no preservatives, they soon lose the fresh crunchiness that gives them the edge over my homemade varieties, and they are all pretty much the same color and shape — beige and square.

Recently, while driving across country, I allowed myself to be talked into buying a bag of fish-shaped cheese crackers for munching on the way. Knowing that I was buying silence in the back seat, I was more than usually tolerant of the ingredients, which as I recall were not particularly nutritious but fairly harmless. No preservatives, I'm sure, or artificial coloring (except what was in the cheese), but probably white flour, salt, some sugar, and a saturated fat.

They were quite a success. Later, while cleaning the crumbs out of the car, I realized that their main appeal to the children was in their shape, remembering them playing "swimming" games with the crackers as I drove along. Why, I thought, couldn't I appeal to that same element in my own cracker making?

I am confident that when the first commercial baking companies began making crackers, they were attempting to duplicate something which had previously been made at home. Yet it is the rare cookbook which today includes recipes for crackers "from scratch", and the rare cook who knows how to make them. The result of this, of course, is that instead of commercial crackers being substitutes for the homemade, the standard has become the ones you buy in the store. And Mommy's efforts are never so colorful, nor so crisp, nor so salty.

So I began anew with my cracker making, and I learned (as I should have know from earlier lessons of this sort) that it is an art, like making a light souffle, or a firm yoghurt, or a sliceable loaf of bread. Do not fret if your first, or your fourth, or your tenth batch of crackers turns out limp, or burned, or less than delectable. If your family is not the forgiving kind, experiment when everyone is out of the house, and save only the successes for sampling. (Our chickens ate well while I was learning.)

Some tips:

Use whole wheat pastry flour rather than regular whole wheat flour. Pastry flour is ground from a softer wheat, has less gluten. That means that overhandling will not toughen your crackers quite so much as it would if they were made with regular whole wheat flour.

If you flour your board before rolling, and you probably will need to, turn each cracker over after cutting it and brush off the excess flour. Tasters who have been raised on die-cut commercial crackers will often turn up their noses at one-sided crackers.

Aim to make your crackers different — special. Use favorite cheeses, cut them with cookie cutters into diamonds, stars, scalloped edged rounds. Sprinkle sesame seeds or poppy seeds over the dough before cutting, then press into the dough lightly with the rolling pin. Turn dough over and do it again (remember, no one-sided crackers). Use toy cookie cutters for soup-sized crackers.

Handle the dough as little as possible. To use the odd-sized pieces after the first cutting, I use the toy cookie cutters from Doña Ana's baking set. Voila — animal crackers. The second rolling always seems to produce tougher results.

The two most important things about making crackers are that you roll them out very thin, and that you dry them thoroughly. It sometimes helps to make the crackers directly on the baking sheet rather than transferring them from table to baking sheet later.

Textures differ depending upon the moisture content of your ingredients, the humidity on the day you make them, and your oven, so experiment until you find the right combination of temperature and time for each batch.

MELBA TOAST

This is made by slicing day old or slighly stale bread very thin and toasting it. My favorite is made from rye bread, since the air bubbles are tiny and the close grain gives more texture to the toast.

Chill the bread before slicing it for easier cutting. Slice bread ¼ inch thick. Place slices side by side on a baking sheet and bake in a slow oven, about 275°F for fifteen or twenty minutes. Turn them over half way through. They should be quite crisp. Store in a tightly sealed container.

WHOLE WHEAT GRAHAM CRACKERS

2 cups whole wheat pastry flour
1 teaspoon baking powder
¼ cup unrefined vegetable oil
½ cup honey
1 tablespoon dark molasses
¼ cup milk

Stir together flour and baking powder, pressing out any lumps. Add oil, honey, and molasses, crumbling between fingers like pastry to blend.

Add as much milk as necessary to make a stiff but workable dough. Roll out on a floured surface to ¼ inch thickness. Cut into squares and prick in several places with a fork (copy a commercial graham cracker for authenticity). Brush lightly with milk. Bake at 350°F for ten to twelve minutes or until golden brown. Store in airtight container.

CHEESE STARS

These originated as animal crackers when I was trying to duplicate the fish crackers after our cross country trip. A star shaped cookie cutter gives them their present distinctive shape. We use white Cheddar cheese, so they are not yellow, like the storebought variety, but no one mistakes their rich cheesy flavor.

1½ cups whole wheat pastry flour
⅓ cup corn oil
1 cup grated sharp Cheddar cheese
¼ teaspoon salt
1 or 2 eggs
Up to ¼ cup water

Stir oil into flour; work in grated cheese and salt. Beat eggs and add, blending dough thoroughly. Add water if necessary to form a soft slightly moist dough (you may not need any if you use both eggs), then roll out very thin and cut into shapes. Bake in a 350°F oven for 8 to 10 minutes. These get crisper as they cool, but sometimes they don't have time to do that.

GROWING YOUR OWN YEAST

A step even further backwards in time than baking bread is growing your own yeast. If you've ever boiled potatoes and left the water sitting in the pan overnight, you know perfectly well how to do it. Or if you have leftover porridge still sitting in the breakfast dishes the next morning (am I giving myself away?), you might have at least noticed that it smells a bit like rising bread.

The first yeasts were undoubtedly discovered the same way (the Sumerians didn't always do their dishes, either), and eventually leavened bread and alcoholic beverages were the result. Yeast of course is now available packaged (and sometimes even preserved — read your label) and convenient in our local markets, and it would be pretty inefficient to return to always growing our own yeast before making a batch of bread.

But you might find it fun, just a few times. And the tastes vary from batch to batch, so that you might even find the results quite worthwhile, as well as educational.

The earliest yeasts came from various sources. The way to grow yeast most predictably is to start with a small quantity of dry yeast and go from there. Homegrown yeast can be used as a starter (save out one cup each time to start the next batch) for years if kept cool and "freshened" frequently (either used to start a new batch or given new food to live on).

Potatoes are a popular place to grow yeasts. My favorite way is to chop three or four medium-sized potatoes (scrub the skins really well and you don't need to peel them) and cook until they fall apart. Drain and mash them, adding enough potato water back in to make three cups of mashed potatoes.

141

Add ¼ cup honey, stir it in well, and cool until just warm to the touch (if the mixture is too hot, it will kill the yeast). Add one cup of starter saved from the last time you made yeast, or a tablespoon of dried yeast dissolved in a cup of lukewarm water. Mix well and leave at room temperature, covered with a wet cloth, for at least eight hours. Take out one cup of starter and use the rest of the yeast mixture to make a batch of four loaves of bread.

You can grow yeast from sprouted grain, too. Take two cups of mixed cereal grains (corn, barley, rice, rye, oats, wheat) and soak them overnight. Drain, and spread on wet paper towels in a shallow baking dish, sprinkling occasionally with water for a day or two, until they begin to sprout. Put through a food mill, mix with water to cover, and boil them until thick. (At this point you have a delicious breakfast cereal, by the way.) Add honey (about ¼ cup) and treat just like the mashed potatoes, above.

The yeast grown in yoghurt, kefir, and cultured buttermilk can also be used to raise bread. To a cup of cultured milk (heated to boiling and cooled to lukewarm if you prefer) add one tablespoon honey, two tablespoons dried yeast, an enough flour to make a fairly stiff batter. Let this dough stand at warm room temperature four or five hours, then add two cups lukewarm water, stir thoroughly, and leave overnight. In the morning, add the remaining ingredients necessary to make your bread, and proceed as usual.

Other mediums can be used to grow yeasts — hops, malt syrup, fruit, and milk. You might find it interesting to experiment with flavors and fragrances of growing yeast. One of the classic early American yeast-growing methods is used to make salt-rising bread, which has been described during its incubation period as smelling like dirty socks. Education and experimentation is always interesting, but not always aesthetic!

Here is a recipe which incorporates the growing of the yeast within it. The result is a sturdy loaf, with a full rich flavor and texture.

GERMAN SCHWARTZBROT (SOUR RYE BREAD)

Starter:

1 quart water in which potatoes have been cooked, cooled
   to lukewarm
2 tablespoons yeast
3 cups rye flour

142

Combine in a large bowl, cover, and leave for 8 to 12 hours. When ready to mix bread, stir in:

2 cups mashed potatoes
1 tablespoon salt
¼ cup malt syrup (also called malted barley syrup; available in supermarkets and health food stores, usualy with molasses)
8 – 10 cups rye flour

Knead in the last of the flour on a floured board, incorporating enough to have a smooth, workable dough. Knead well, until dough is smooth and elastic. Cover with a damp cloth and let rise one hour. Make into two medium or three small loaves, cover with a damp cloth, and let rise 30 minutes.

Bake at 350°F for one hour with a pan of water in the bottom of the oven (this is to try and duplicate the German brick ovens). Turn out on a rack to cool, and when thoroughly cool slice it very thin, spread with a little fresh butter, and prepare your taste buds for a treat.

SAUSAGES AND DRIED MEATS

Making your own sausages is not difficult if you own a mixer with a sausage stuffer, or know someone who does. Several of us got together last winter to make sausages and it was really enjoyable. Similar, I suspect, to old-time quilting bees. We felt very self-sufficient and competent filling casings with our mixtures of herbs and meat.

If you have access to freshly butchered meat or some which you know has not been treated with nitrates (or antibiotics or stilbesterol or any of the other chemicals injected into many of today's meat animals), you might want to make your own, too. Grind pork or a mixture of pork and beef with a blend of sage, thyme, salt, pepper, and marjoram, stuff into casings, twisting every five or six inches, tie off, and freeze.

Another way to preserve meat in your own home without the use of chemicals is to make jerky. Jerky was originally made with heavy brine and lots of herbs and spices to cover the strong flavor of wild game, but you can dry beef, too, and adjust the seasonings to suit your palate.

The easiest way is to partially thaw some frozen round steak, chuck steak, or other inexpensive cut of meat, and cut it horizontally, with the grain of the meat, into ¼ inch slices. Cut these into strips, removing fat, place on racks for air circulation, and dry in your oven at the lowest setting. Turn after three hours and dry for three more hours. Turn off oven and leave meat in overnight. This jerky is brittle, and can be kept in jars just about indefinitely. For more flavor, salt or season meat with herbs before drying.

For sausage, jerky, and salt-brine recipes, check out the following how-to books: *The Up-With-Wholesome, Down-With-Store-Bought Book of Recipes and Household Formulas*, by Yvonne Young Tarr, and *Old-Fashioned Recipe Book*, by Carla Emery.

WHY SWEETEN SWEET FRUIT? MAKING JAMS AND JELLIES WITH HONEY

In recent years many people have been influenced by such books as *Sweet and Dangerous*, by Peter H. Wyden, and *Sugar Blues*, by William Dufty, and have made some real changes in their family's eating habits with regard to the intake of refined sugar. As a culture, we consume far too much sugar, and doctors are now telling us that sugar is the agent responsible not only for tooth decay, but also for obesity, hypoglycemia, and coronary disease.

Even with the best of intentions, however, many of us who have substituted honey for sugar in recipes all year long, and have successfully reduced our family's intake of cookies, candies, and soft drinks, will during canning season trek to the grocery store and bring home twenty pounds of white sugar to use in processing the year's fruit. Some of us try to substitute honey into bottled fruit recipes, but no one I know has until recently had much success with eliminating sugar from jams or jellies.

One of the main reasons that it is difficult to remove or replace sugar in jams and jellies is that the jelling process usually *requires* sugar. The chemical interaction between pectin, sugar, and acid is what causes fruit syrup to stiffen, and commonly-used commercial pectins (MCP, Sure-Jell, etc.) require even more sugar to attain a jell than do the natural fruit pectins utilized in the old-fashioned cook-down methods. Unfortunately, however, if honey is substituted for sugar in the old recipes, the extra liquid takes longer to cook out, and extensive cooking of honey results in darkening and loss of flavor.

The secret seems to be in the type of pectin used. One of my friends discovered something called low-methoxyl pectin in a mail-order catalogue, and we made last year's jam with it, using no sugar at all, only a small amount of honey.

144

Low-methoxyl pectin uses a calcium salt to form a jell instead of sugar, and so it allows us to make jam and jelly with honey, or with artificial sweetener, or with no sweetening at all, if desired. This pectin was located by Euell Gibbons' brother, a diabetic, and he experimented with it in the production of his own preserves.

Low-methoxyl pectin has been used for years by commercial canners, but now can be purchased from some health food stores, along with the calcium salts needed to stiffen the fruit. If you cannot find low-methoxyl pectin in your area, write to Walnut Acres, Penns Creek, Pennsylvania 17862, for their catalogue.

FRESH-SWEET FRUIT JAM

Choose fully ripe fresh fruit, rinse well and simmer until quite soft in as little water as possible. (Remove seeds before cooking or put the cooked fruit through a sieve to remove seeds and skins.) Measure your finished pulp, place it in a large saucepan over low heat and bring just to a boil.

CALCIUM SOLUTION (will be needed later)

Dissolve ⅛ teaspoon calcium disulphate in ¼ cup water.   Set aside.

Procedure:

Measure into a mixing bowl 1 tablespoon light honey, ½ teaspoon of low-methoxyl pectin, and 1 tablespoon juice from pan *for each cup of fruit*, and mix thoroughly. Pour this mixture into the boiling fruit and stir thoroughly until the pectin is completely dissolved.

Taste for sweetness, and add more honey if necessary, or lemon juice for tartness, or any spices you wish. When you are happy with your jam, add one teaspoon of the calcium solution (see above proportion) *for each cup of fruit*, and quickly stir until mixed.

At this point you can pour the jam into sterilized jars, seal and set aside to cool, or you may remove it from the heat and place a tiny amount in a saucer in the refrigerator to test the jell. If it is too stiff, add a little juice or water to the pot; if too runny, add another teaspoon of the calcium solution.

Be sure to seal the jam properly with two-piece sterilized lids in sterilized jars, because the omission of the large amount of sugar leaves the jam open to spoilage if it is merely paraffined.

A second method of sugarless jam was taught to me by a friend, Dorrie Adams. Originally discovered in *You Can Can With Honey*, a pamphlet by Nancy Cosper, McKenzie Bridge, Oregon 97401, her recipe uses a seaweed thickener called agar. Dorrie's version of strawberry jam, which can be adjusted for other fruit, calls for 1 cup of mild honey for each 8 cups of crushed fruit. Heat fruit just to boiling, stir in 4 tablespoons agar flakes (or 2 tablespoons agar powder) and 2 tablespoons lemon juice. Boil 2 minutes and pack into sterile jars; seal.

Because this jam requires very little cooking, it may retain more nutrients, and certainly retains the flavor of the raw fruit. A drawback is that the jam must be refrigerated or frozen if it is to be kept longer than a couple of months. However, the flavor may compensate for the inconvenience — it certainly does in our house.

Other jam and jelly ideas, as well as many recipes for preserving food without sugar, may be found in *Putting It Up With Honey*, by Susan Geiskopf.

MAKE YOUR OWN BUTTER

The fat content of cream differs from milking to milking, just like the color and Vitamin A content of the resulting butter. I have obtained as much as 1½ pounds of butter from a quart of cream, and as little as ¾ pound. So it is difficult to say how much it costs to make your own butter. Over a period of a year, however, I feel that the butter we eat has cost about a dollar a pound.

The reason that this is possible is that I visit a dairy once a week and buy cream by the quart. The dairy also sells raw milk, which is the original reason I began going there, but the cream is pasteurized, and could be purchased from an ordinary dairy for probably just as low a price as I pay. Contact your local agricultural representative, or look in the yellow pages under milk, or dairies, or similar headings. They still exist, even in the middle of some cities.

For the sake of experimentation, you can use ordinary whipping cream from your supermarket. Be sure to buy cream which has no additives, and has not been "ultra-pasteurized", or your butter will be no better than the type you can purchase commercially. Butter can be churned from sweet cream or cream which has spoiled, although butter made from the soured cream should be salted.

You can make butter in the small quantities we do without a churn. Use your blender at the lowest speed, or a quart jar. Experiment with about a cup of cream at a time, perhaps working up to larger

146

amounts later. The cream should be cool, but not too cold. Blend at the lowest speed until the cream thickens and sticks to the sides of the container; if you are using a jar, hold it by the ends to keep from warming the cream too much, and shake it for five to ten minutes.

If your cream stops moving, either in the jar or the blender, add cool water or milk (up to ½ the original quantity of cream), and push the cream away from the sides of the container with a rubber scraper. Continue to shake or blend until the fat separates from the buttermilk in clumps about the size of corn kernels.

Strain through a sieve (reserve the buttermilk for drinking or soups; it is not cultured and won't raise pancakes unless your cream is sour), wash with a cup or so of cool water, then press with a wooden spoon to remove the liquid (press into a bowl, not a sieve, or you'll lose the butter through the holes).

Repeat with the remainder of the cream until you have your week's batch done, then pack into small containers (we use paper cups), cover with foil or waxed paper, and freeze until needed. If not salted (we don't salt ours), this butter will turn rancid at room temperature, so keep it refrigerated until shortly before each use.

If you decide to salt your butter, do so after pressing out the liquid. Beat in the salt thoroughly, and leave at room temperature for at least an hour, then beat again to remove any graininess which might result from the salt crystals.

ICE CREAM

Last summer brought a new joy to my life — hand-cranked ice cream. Oh, I've tasted it before, at birthday parties and special events in the lives of my friends, but somehow I have always managed to be busy holding a baby or helping in the kitchen, and never got involved in the real business of turning the crank on the ice cream freezer.

If you talk with the older people in your life, you'll undoubtedly find quite a few who have fond memories of family and friends circling the old ice cream barrel, talking and laughing while someone turned the crank and someone else sat on the top to keep it from jiggling. Sometimes songs were sung, sometimes nonsense chants repeated to give the turner a meter to his job.

One of my students told us about her grandparents, who ran a catering service. They cranked all their own ice cream, and she remembers it with pleasure, not drudgery. A close friend remembers Sunday summer nights when the whole neighborhood would collect at someone's house to crank together and sit on the porch as the sun finally set, spooning the flavor of the week into their mouths.

Still another friend, and this one not yet thirty, links all celebrations to the ritual of home frozen ice cream. Perhaps it is the surplus of hands (and arms) around their family gatherings (she's the eldest of seven children) that has led them to include this treat in each of their feasts. So when they think back to birthdays, graduations, shed-raisings, or the birth of a child, they also think of the togetherness of that cranking, cranking, cranking.

Electric ice cream freezers are simply not the same. First, the texture of electrically turned cream doesn't approach the creaminess and smoothness of the hand-made variety, but second, and perhaps the real reason that hand freezers are reviving in popularity, is that simply plugging in a freezer is a lonely job, not at all so companionable as cheerful cranking. And ice cream, after all, is a social custom, not just a food.

Iced cream desserts have been a part of Western history since the thirteenth century, when Marco Polo is believed to have returned from China with some recipes for flavored ices. The earliest versions were made from fresh snow mixed with fruit and spices, and later cream and milk were added. English colonists probably brought recipes with them, and some of the earliest colonial cookery books contain ices and ice creams. Americans now eat an average of 23 quarts of ice cream a year, by far the largest amount eaten in the world.

Most of our tradition in ice cream has been a home-based one, that picture changing in 1904 when an enterprising fellow served ice cream cones at the world's fair. Shortly after that, soda fountains introduced sodas, sundaes, and other ways of serving this dessert, and by the middle of this century, commercial production of ice cream was a big business.

Sadly for those of us who really like old-fashioned ice cream, the commercial varieties have succumbed to the shortcuts and techniques

so common to the food industry, and now along with a dazzling array of colors and flavors offered in supermarkets and ice cream parlors come the numerous ingredients utilized to keep the product fresh, hard, smooth, and palatable after shipping. In addition to the basic ingredients of cream, milk, eggs and sugar, today's commercial ice cream may contain cooked cereal, numerous stabilizing and thickening agents, emulsifiers, dissolving agents, artificial coloring, artificial flavoring, and chemicals to make sure each batch is identical to each other batch (how dull!).

Ice cream manufacturers belong to that elite group of food people who are not required by law to list their ingredients on the label. Personally, I feel that there should be no exceptions to the ingredient disclosure laws — putting the contents of a food product on the label does not guarantee that our food will be any more healthful, but at least we'll know what we are getting. Imagine the discomfort of someone allergic to wheat when she/he discovers that the ice cream purchased in good faith uses cooked wheat bran for a filler!

I recommend that for regular ice cream purchases one explore a large natural food store, where excellent ice creams can be found which are made with honey *instead* of sugar (not in addition to, as some of the more widely advertised brands are), and with only natural ingredients, fully listed on the label. And for a special taste treat and a wonderful time, let me recommend that you try making your own ice cream once in a while.

Hand cranked ice cream freezers come in a wide variety of sizes and prices. You can get away for as little as $15 or spend as much as $70. My favorite type uses a wooden bucket to hold the ice, and has multiple actions from the movement of the dasher and the rotation of the cream holder. You can see into the ice cream compartment in some types, too, which is interesting for the people turning the crank, and motivates them to keep working.

The basic method is to make a custard of cream, eggs (sometimes), sweeteners, milk, and flavorings (which can be fresh fruit or spices), then place it in the center of a pan full of ice and salt. The old recipes have you place a bucket of custard in the center of a washtub of ice; the modern ice cream freezers provide a removable cylinder for the mixture, and a bucket with attachable handle for the ice. The salt melts the ice, lowering the temperature as it does so. Turning the ice cream (slowly and evenly, never too fast) as it freezes incorporates air and prevents ice crystals from forming. Many recipes exist; try this basic one which requires no cooking, and alter it to suit your family's taste.

CREAMY FRENCH VANILLA ICE CREAM

In a blender container or medium bowl combine:

4 eggs
1 quart fresh cream
1 cup whole milk
1 cup noninstant powdered milk

Blend or beat until foamy. Add while blending:

1/2 cup mild honey
1/8 teaspoon salt
1 tablespoon vanilla

Pour into freezer cylinder of a hand crank ice cream freezer, and add whole milk up to half full point (for a 2 quart container you will need to halve the recipe). Close and freeze according to freezer instructions.

If you have no ice cream freezer it is possible to halve or quarter this recipe, blend or beat thoroughly, then freeze it in ice cube trays, removing and beating three times, one-half hour apart.

Fresh fruit puree (up to two or three cups) can be added before the final milk is poured in. Decrease vanilla to one teaspoon if you use fruit.

150

SAUCES AND DRESSINGS

The sauces and dressings used in any household are a fairly individual selection, but so many of them purchased from supermarkets contain artificial ingredients that are necessary for packaging and shipping but not for the good flavor.

We began to make our own salad dressings using the prepackaged seasonings when we learned about preservatives and heat processing in vegetable oils. However, once we began reading the seasoning labels, we moved the next step, to creating the seasoning combinations ourselves. We read the ingredients on the ones we liked best, and began by combining some of those ingredients together. Eventually we arrived at a few favorites, and they have evolved over the years.

I give you this process in some detail only to make the point that it is a process, not a recipe or a formula. Every brand of barbecue sauce or salad dressing is discrete; if you are trying to duplicate something you know your family likes, you will need to experiment. We don't measure as much as we did at first. Trying to write a recipe for barbecue sauce was very difficult. We pour together soy sauce, oil, honey, dry mustard, ketchup, and salt and pepper. Then we taste it. We rarely make the same sauce twice, and if we are out of some of the ingredients we wing it.

However, for guidelines here are a few of our basic ones. Take them as places to start, and work them from there to something special which fits you and your family.

BASIC CREAM SAUCE

This sauce can be used as the base for cheese sauce (add grated cheese), creamed vegetables (add cut corn or chopped spinach, etc.), creamed soup (add more liquid), or souffles (use 3 tablespoons each of butter and flour).

    2 tablespoons butter
    2 tablespoons whole wheat pastry flour
    1 cup liquid (water, milk, stock)

Melt butter in heavy skillet. Stir in flour. Add liquid a bit at a time, stirring constantly. Keep temperature quite low as you do this, and continue to stir and cook over the low temperature until sauce thickens. If lumps should develop which you cannot press out with a wooden spoon, you can pour sauce into a blender and liquify. However, you sacrifice texture.

FAST PASTA SAUCE

1 large can tomato sauce
1 cup cooked brown rice
1 cup cooked vegetables (limas, squash, onions, peas)
1 teaspoon marjoram
1 teaspoon parsley
1 teaspoon oregano
1 teaspoon Vigor Cup

Puree sauce with rice and vegetables in blender; heat with seasonings and simmer for five to fifteen minutes. Serve. This doesn't have so rich a flavor as a sauce which has been cooking all day, but it serves just fine when you're in a hurry.

TERIYAKI SAUCE

½ cup tamari soy sauce
⅛ cup vinegar
⅛ cup wine
1 tablespoon honey
dash freshly ground pepper

Shake all ingredients together (it helps to warm the honey first). This will separate between uses. Shake vigorously before using.

BARBECUE SAUCE

This can start with the Teriyaki Sauce if you have some made. Just add ketchup and mustard powder to taste, then add about ⅓ the amount of sauce in oil.

½ cup tamari soy sauce
¼ cup vegetable oil
¼ cup vinegar
¼ cup honey
¼ cup ketchup
1 teaspoon dry mustard powder
sale
pepper
(garlic)

Shake together. Brush on meat before and during cooking. Can also be used as a marinade.

OIL/VINEGAR
For an oil and vinegar type of dressing, combine one part vinegar or lemon juice to two parts unrefined vegetable oil. Herbs which can be added for flavoring include sage, marjoram, basil, thyme, tarragon, salt and pepper — you may have other favorites.

If you are going to make a dressing in a jar rather than at the table, pulverize the herbs in a mortar and pestle or in your hands first, then add a small amount of water to the dressing to help in rehydrating them.

You might also enjoy reading the section devoted to salads.

CREAMY — BLUE CHEESE OR OTHER

A nice base can be made in a blender container of one part mayonnaise, one part yoghurt and one part cream cheese. For Roquefort or blue cheese dressing, substitute one part of that cheese for the cream cheese.

You can then go where you wish with this dressing. Add ketchup and mustard and it's a French dressing; lemon juice, honey and celery seed and you can use it for coleslaw.

MAYONNAISE

You can buy good quality mayonnaise made with unrefined vegetable oils (or at least ones without preservatives) and with no sugar. However, this dressing is easier to make in a blender than you can imagine, and should you run out occasionally, it's nice to be able to do it yourself.

In a blender, place:

1 egg or 2 yolks and 1 white
1 teaspoon dry mustard
½ teaspoon salt
1 teaspoon honey
¼ cup vegetable oil

Blend, and add while blending:

½ cup vegetable oil
¼ cup lemon juice

Slowly, while still blending, add:

½ cup salad oil

Stir mixture down (after stopping blender) if necessary. Blend until thick. Refrigerate. Use within two or three days.

A THOUGHT ABOUT
NATURAL REMEDIES

It always surprises me when I walk into the sickroom of one of my friends' children and discover cough medicine, decongestant, and antibiotic bottles by the bedside — all brightly proclaiming their artificial coloring. I don't mean to sound smug — for years we also used the standard sugared, flavored, and colored cold and flu remedies — but let me propose an alternative.

None of us need artificial colorings. We can intellectually handle browns, greys, and other muddy colors which are often the result of blending fruit juices, vegetables, or even pharmaceuticals, and do not need to have our beverages, foods, or medicines candy-apple red or jello green. Many children (and adults) react strongly to chemical compounds used for colorings, and some people show reactions when their defenses are down, if not at other times. In other words, at the very least, artificial colorings are unnecessary; at worst, such as during illness, they can be downright harmful.

I discovered this firsthand. After a painful ear infection in infancy, my son John developed ear congestion with each succeeding cold. In an attempt to ward off future infections, we began a regimen of decongestants and antibiotics at the first sign of a sniffle for the whole next winter. And with each cold, John would break out in an angry rash and the cranky fussies.

One day I realized that I was feeding him medicine which no way resembled the kind of food he ate — I did not apply the same rules to it as I did to supermarket fare (no colorings, no flavorings, no sugar, no preservatives). If his decongestant came in a bottle marked "Orange Juice: artificially colored, artificially flavored, contains cane sugar and corn syrup sweeteners, a preservative and two flavor enhancers" I wouldn't buy it. So why was I purchasing it to feed him when he was ill?

Obviously, because I hadn't thought it through before, and because I didn't know there were any alternatives. A trip through any pharmacy will reveal dozens of national brands of pain relievers and cold remedies developed for children. We have removed aspirin from many of the formulas and replaced it with acetaminophen, but have made no noticeable dent in the colorings, flavorings, or sweeteners. Vitamin pills are another area of concern, but at least there are naturally colored and flavored alternatives for those in some stores.

A discussion with my children's pediatrician, however, and a later talk with our local pharmacist, elicited an alternative for John. There are one or two brands of adult decongestants on the market which are free of antihistimines and side effects, such as drowsiness and upset stomachs. I have explored these in the past for my own use during pregnancy and nursing, when the use of any drugs should be limited to near zero. There are also numerous fairly safe pain relievers, aspirins, or aspirin substitutes, intended for adults and not flavored, colored, or sweetened.

With the help of the pharmacist, we calculated the correct dosage of each of these medicines (the same procedure was later taken with the antibiotic prescribed by the doctor), pulverized the appropriate fraction of the pills and mixed the powder with a teaspoon of honey. This was easily accepted by baby John.

We were rewarded for our efforts by the obvious absence of rash for his entire illness, and much less fussiness and tears. We've continued through the years, never again buying the syrups which are pushed so strongly for children. When he learned to swallow pills, we purchased empty gelatin capsules from an herb shop and filled them with the appropriate pulverized pharmaceutical. I dislike giving medicines at all, and restrict even the use of aspirin and acetaminophen to severe earaches and other pain. However, when it is necessary for him to sleep or otherwise to need help healing his body, I feel that giving him pure medicine, instead of candied remedies, is at least a compromise I can live with.

The moral of this whole sermon is that we should look all around us, into all aspects of our lives, and seek the natural, the more wholesome. How about toothpaste? (There are many made from clay and herbs.) Antacids? (Try milk or yoghurt.) Eye wash? Sore throat? (Slippery elm tea has been successful for generations.)

All around us are highly advertised chemical solutions to physical problems. Let's try to minimize those kinds of solutions, and certainly when we decide that they are warranted, avoid using the candied versions. Excellent books about herbs and natural remedies can now be found in libraries and bookstores. I look in one of those before (often instead of) going to the pharmacy.

MY MAMA'S LEMON TEA

A home remedy my mother taught me, this lemon tea soothes the worst sore throat, and helps to loosen phlegm.

Into a teapot or other similar vessel, slice three washed lemons thinly. Spoon a tablespoon or so of honey over the lemons; cover with boiling water. Steep for five to ten minutes, stirring to blend flavors. Sweeten if necessary to taste.

BIBLIOGRAPHY

Airola, Paavo. *How To Get Well.* Health Plus, 1974.

Bumgarner, Marlene Anne. *The Book of Whole Grains.* St. Martin's Press, 1976.

Cooper, Jane. *Love at First Bite.* Knopf, 1977.

Cosper, Nancy. *You Can Can With Honey.* McKenzie Bridge, Oregon 97401, 1976.

Davis, Adelle, *Let's Cook It Right.* Harcourt Brace Jovanovich (Signet Edition, 1970)

_____, *Let's Have Healthy Children.* Harcourt Brace Jovanovich (Signet Edition, 1972)

Dworkin, Stan and Floss. *Bake Your Own Bread and be Healthier.* Holt, Rinehart & Winston, 1972.

_____, *Natural Snacks and Sweets.* Rodale Press, 1974.

Dufty, William. *Sugar Blues.* Warner Books, 1975.

Emery, Carla. *Old Fashioned Recipe Book.* Kendrick, Idaho, 1976.

Feingold, Ben F. *Why Your Child is Hyperactive.* Random House, 1974.

Geiskopf, Susan. *Putting it Up With Honey.* Quicksilver Publications, 1979.

Goldbeck, Nikki & David. *Supermarket Handbook.* New American Library, 1976.

Hunter, Beatrice Trum. *Factbook on Yoghurt, Kefir & Other Milk Cultures.* Keats Publishing Co., 1973.

_____, *Factbook on Food Additives and Your Health.* Keats Publishing Co., 1980.

Jacobson, Michael. *Eater's Digest.* Anchor Books, 1976.

Kinderlehrer, Jane. *Confessions of a Sneaky Organic Cook.* Rodale, 1971.

Kinmont, Vikki. *Simple Foods for the Pack.* Sierra Club Books, 1976.

Lansky, Vicki. *Taming of the C.A.N.D.Y. Monster.* Meadowbrook Press, 1978.

La Leche League International. *The Womanly Art of Breastfeeding.* Franklin Park, Illinois. 1971.

Lappe', Frances Moore. *Diet For a Small Planet.* Ballantine, 1971.

Mother Earth News, P.O. Box 70, Hendersonville, North Carolina.

Newman, Nanette. *Fun Food Factory.* Harmony Books, 1976.

Nutrition Search, Inc. *Nutrition Alamanac.* McGraw Hill, 1979.

Organic Gardening and Farming, Rodale Press, Emmaus, Pennsylvania.

Pryor, Karen. *Breastfeeding Your Baby.* Harper & Row, 1973.

Reuben, David, M.D. *Save Your Life Diet.* Ballantine, 1975.

Rodale Press. *Natural Breakfast Book.* 1973.

Robertson, Laurel, Carol Flinders and Bronwen Godfrey. *Laurel's Kitchen.* Nilgiri Press, 1976.

Rombauer, Irma S. and Marion Rombauer Becker. *Joy of Cooking.* Bobbs-Merrill Co. Revised Edition, 1971.

Scott, Cyril. *Crude Black Molasses, The Natural Wonder Food.* Lust Publications, 1973.

Shurtleff, William and Akiko Aoyagi. *The Book of Tofu.* Autumn Press, 1976.

Smith, Lendon H. *Improving Your Child's Behavior Chemistry.* Prentice-Hall, 1976.

_____, *Feed Your Kids Right.* McGraw Hill, 1979.

Soman, Robert O. *Natural Foods Ice Cream Book.* Pyramid Book, 1975.

Stoner, Carol Hupping, Ed. *Stocking Up.* Rodale Press, 1977 rev ed.

Tarr, Yvonne Young. *Super Easy Step by Step Cheese-making Book*. Vintage Press Random House, 1975.

_____, *The Up-With-Wholesome, Down-With-Store-Bought Book of Recipes and Household Formulas*. Random House, 1975.

Tyree, Marion Cabell, Ed. *Housekeeping in Old Virginia*. John P. Morton and Co. 1879.

United States Department of Agriculture Handbook No. 8. *Composition of Foods*. USDA, 1963.

Wade, Carlson. *Book of Bran*. B.J. Publishers, 1976.

Wallace, Aubrey. *Natural Foods for the Trail*. Vegelsang Press, P.O. Box 757 Yosemite, CA 95389, 1977.

Yudkin, John M.D. *Sweet and Dangerous*. Wyden Publishers, 1972.

APPENDIX
SOURCES OF SUPPLY

Day Fresh Wheat Germ
   Imperial Distributors
   Box 745 C
   Pasadena, CA 91104

Earthwonder Natural Meals-in-a-Box
   Earthwonder Farm
   BlueEye, MO 65611

Low Methoxyl Pectin
   Walnut Acres
   Penns Creek, PA 17862

Malt Powder
   Giusto's Specialty Food Company
   241 E. Harris Ave.
   South San Francisco, CA 94080

Mouli grater, sprouters, yoghurt makers, blenders, other equipment
   Basic Living Products
   2990 7th Street
   Berkeley, CA 94710

Natural Food Backpack Dinners
   P.O. Box 532
   Corvallis, OR 97330

Tofu
   Dairy case of large supermarket or delicatessen
   Or check your telephone directory yellow pages for Tofu Shops

Vigor Cup powdered soup mix
   2740 Grand Avenue
   Bellmore, NY 11710

INDEX

160

163

ORGANIC COOKING FOR (not-so-organic) MOTHERS
by
Marlene Anne Bumgarner

At last, a really good natural foods cookbook
written by a mother . .... for mothers

Rich with how-to's and recipes that take
the mystery out of natural foods
and don't rely on expensive or
hard-to-find ingredients

Beautifully illustrated by
Maryanna Kingman and
Jean McManis

preface by
Lendon H. Smith, M.D.

NATURAL LIVING ASSOCIATES, P.O. Box 1326, Morgan Hill, CA 95037

_____ copies of ORGANIC COOKING FOR (not-so-organic) MOTHERS ($4.95)
_____ copies of THE BOOK OF WHOLE GRAINS ($5.95)

THE BOOK OF WHOLE GRAINS: THE GRAIN-BY-GRAIN GUIDE TO COOKING,
GROWING, AND GRINDING WHOLE CEREALS, NUTS, PEAS, AND BEANS, by
Marlene Anne Bumgarner. A super practical handbook for preparing your own cracked,
cereals and flours, with over 250 specific recipes for everything from appetizers and
breads to vegetarian delights.

_____ subscription to Natural Living Newsline ($6.00 per year) _____

NAME _____   California residents ADD
                                            6% sales tax
                                            Postage and handling
ADDRESS _____   ($.65 for Organic Cooking)
                                            ($.75 for Book of Whole Grains) _____

CITY _____ STATE _____ ZIP _____   TOTAL ENCLOSED is my check for _____

165

The manuscript for this book was prepared on magnetic disk at Cottage Computing in Oakland, California using a WORDSTAR Word Processing System. Type was set at Abracadabra Typesetting in Palo Alto, California, on an Itek quadritek machine programmed in FORTH.

Pasteup took place at Country Wordshop, Ramona, California, mostly in the living room, with the help of five children. A-D Graphics, Poway, did the printing; binding was done at Valley Reproduction, in San Jose, California.

Sincerest thanks to Richard and Frog Barnhart, Dave Kilbridge, Sue Olson, Maryanna Kingman, and Jean McManis, who volunteered many hours to make this book happen.